Managing the
Generation Mix:
From Collision
to Collaboration

Carolyn A. Martin, Ph.D.
& Bruce Tulgan

P7-EEZ-383

HRD PRESS
Amherst, Massachusetts

Published by: HRD Press, Inc.
                 22 Amherst Road
                 Amherst, MA 01002
                 800-822-2801 (U.S. and Canada)
                 413-253-3488
                 413-253-3490 (fax)
                 http://www.hrdpress.com

ISBN: 0-87425-659-3

Cover design by Eileen Klockars
Editorial and production services by Mary George
Printed in Canada

In memory of John Martin,
a member of the Greatest Generation,
whose life of quiet bravery inspired
his Boomer children to succeed
far beyond his fondest dreams.

Table of Contents

Acknowledgments

AS ALWAYS, we are grateful to the thousands of people who, over the years, have shared their workplace experiences with us, giving voice and vitality to our ongoing research at RainmakerThinking, Inc. Topping the list for this project are the audiences in our Generation Mix workshops who defined the major issues that divide as well as unite an age-diverse workforce; the subscribers to our online newsletter who kept us current with their insights by faithfully responding to our Question of the Month; and the extraordinary people we met every day, at meetings and conventions, in restaurants and airports, face to face and in cyberspace, who confirmed that age is, indeed, the latest diversity issue.

We are also indebted to the many others who lent their assistance to our research for *Managing the Generation Mix,* especially the following: the articulate Gen Yers at David Douglas High School in Portland, Oregon, who, along with their entrepreneurial Gen X teacher, Mr. Eric Johannsen, told us what they expect from managers; Brenda Meyer and the members of the Douglas County Employer Council in Roseburg, Oregon, who recognized the importance of age-diversity issues long before anyone else; Cynthia Conrad at RainmakerThinking, who compiled the recommended resources list and whose regular research and editing contributes so much to all our publications.

To the rest of our colleagues at RainmakerThinking, especially Jeff Coombs, Mark Kurber, Peggy Urbanowicz, Colleen Keating, Susan Ciemniewski, Joe Engwer, Dr. Donald Gibson, and Heather Neely, thank you for your encouragement, hard work, and the valuable contributions you make to this enterprise every day.

Many thanks as well to our friend and publisher, Bob Carkhuff, and his staff at HRD Press. Bob has continuously supported our work since the early days. The partnership we maintain with HRD Press is critical to our ability to reach inside organizations of every shape and size and make them even better than they already are. Special thanks, too, to Mary George for her consistently excellent editing and production work and to Eileen Klockars for her eye-catching cover designs.

As co-authors, we also have our respective debts of gratitude to express.

From Carolyn: Thank you to my Silent Generation friends and colleagues Betty McQuilken, Helen Green, Don Wright, Jack Moore, and Paul Enberg, all of whom helped me shed preconceived notions about this dedicated, often outrageous cohort; to Marilyn MacGregor,

Ph.D., a Boomer whose insightful reading of this manuscript pushed me to clarify my thinking on key issues; and to my best friend, Kathy Richard, a practical "Joneser" who challenges my Boomer idealism every day.

From Bruce: Thank you from the bottom of my heart to my wise family and friends, who are the center of my universe. As always, I reserve my deepest thanks for my wife, the brilliant Dr. Debby Applegate.

Introduction

THERE'S NO DOUBT ABOUT IT: The newest diversity issue on the block is generational diversity. Age has taken its place beside gender, race, and culture as a way to define what binds some groups of people together and drives other groups absolutely crazy. If you have parents who grew up during the Great Depression, siblings who witnessed the turbulent 60s and Watergate, or teenagers who zip effortlessly around the Internet, you know all about generational clashes and collisions.

When it comes to the workplace, it's no surprise that age is "up." On one hand, the aging U.S. population is working longer and longer. On the other, demand for new young talent is skyrocketing. And in the middle, organizations are downsizing, upsizing, merging, and acquisitioning at such a rate that people of all ages are thrown together more quickly and more intensely than ever before.

Scrambling to respond to an unpredictable, market-driven economy, most organizations have found themselves in a quandary. They've finally figured out how to recruit young talents, only to watch them clash with older, seasoned employees over issues like work ethic, respect for authority, dress codes, and every work arrangement imaginable. And they're not sure what to do about it.

We hear cross-generational complaints every day, from people of every age in every industry. For example:

- "No one wants to pay their dues any more," complains a 56-year-old. "They want the corner office right now without earning it—or sacrificing for it. These young people just don't have our work ethic."

- "If I could change one thing about my job," says a twentysomething, "it would be the corporate people I have to deal with day in and day out— stuffy, been-there-longer-than-God types, dead set against any type of change."

- A 19-year-old explains: "The oldest boss doesn't like kids. He doesn't want to talk to you. He grunts in acknowledgment that you're there. He thinks what older people are doing is more im-portant."

- "We've been receiving training in our office on all kinds of diversity issues," a 62-year-old legal assistant confides after butting heads with a 26-year-old colleague. "But I never knew age was one of them. I do now!"

Age Is "One of Them"

Age, indeed, is "one of them," and managers like you are tackling age-related challenges every day. Some of them tell us they're having difficulty integrating young workers into their "traditional" workplace. Others claim they can't motivate older staffers close to retirement to learn anything new. A fiftysomething supervisor wants to get rid of her stodgy peers and work only with enthusiastic twentysomethings. A thirtysomething store manager complains his new teen hires have no sense of customer service.

After our extensive work on Generations X and Y, the next management challenge in the new economy was obvious: how to handle this "generation mix." What insights, skills, and best practices would managers need in order to steer colliding beliefs, values, and attitudes toward collaborative team efforts? The answers that we discovered are presented in this book, the latest in RainmakerThinking's series of pocket guides published by HRD Press.

Generational Definitions, and a Difference of Opinion

Most experts would agree that there are four distinct generational cohorts in the workplace today; however, many disagree about their exact parameters. Some

Civilian Non-Institutional Workforce
RainmakerThinking Estimates 2001

TOTAL: 143 Million

Cohort (Birth Years)	Approx. #	Approx. %
Gen Yers (1978–85)	20 million	14%
Gen Xers (1965–77)	42 million	29.5%
Cuspers (1963–64)	7 million	5%
Baby Boomers (1946–62)	58 million	40.5%
Silents		
(before 1946)	16 million	11%
(before 1931)	1.7 million	

demographers call the oldest workers "The Veterans" and set their birth years between 1922 and 1943. Others label them "The Silent Generation," with birth years set between 1925 and 1942. Some say the Baby Boom began in 1943 with "Victory Children"; others start it in 1946, after the end of World War II. Some claim that Gen Xers (or "Thirteeners") were born between 1961 and 1983, and Generation Yers (or the "Millennials") between 1984 and 2003. Others narrow the gap to 1965 through 1977 for Xers, and 1978 through 1985 for Yers.

Of course, every day we talk to people who rebel at being put into any age-group category at all. "I'm *not* a Gen Xer!" a 24-year-old bristles. A fortysomething accuses us of gross stereotyping. "This [generational] pigeonholing is as bad as racial stereotyping," he rages.

A 57-year-old entrepreneur confides, "I'm more like an Xer than a Boomer in my thinking. And I'm proud of it." Fortysomething writer Jonathan Pontell argues that he and his peers belong to "Generation Jones," some 49 million Americans born between 1954 and 1965 who identify neither with idealistic Boomers nor with cynical Xers.

Perhaps the truth is that generations are in the eye of the age holder, and there are, after all, five billion generations—one for each unique individual living on the planet. Yet, over the past eight years, through our extensive work with hundreds of organizations—from Fortune 500 companies to trade associations to small businesses—we've discovered that it is still meaningful to talk in terms of generational identities. Coming of age during key socio-historical events still influences how each cohort reacts and responds in the workplace—and, subsequently, why they collide with one another.

Collaboration Is a Business Imperative

Today, turning that collision into collaboration is a business imperative. Why? It all comes down to numbers: There simply aren't enough Gen Xers and Gen Yers to take the place of all the Silents and Boomers who will retire during the next five to 15 years. According to some leading estimates, by 2008 the U.S. economy will offer nearly 161 million jobs to 155 million workers. The Hudson Institute predicts that the supply of skilled labor in the United States will not catch up to the demand until 2050. So every skilled worker of every age will be needed in every successful enterprise.

"You're too young" and *"You're too old"* are already moot points that need to be eliminated immediately from your hiring criteria. Who cares if someone is 19 or 59? Can they do the work that needs to get done today? Can they learn the skills necessary to become up-to-date knowledge workers who consistently add value to the workplace and to their own lives? Do they have the willingness to leverage their talents and expertise in collaborative efforts?

A 58-year-old computer expert in the mail-advertising industry explains: "Employers need to realize that some of us older professionals have grown children. We may be divorced or widowed, and we have incredible skills and the time to work. And we want to work."

At the other end of the spectrum, a 20-year-old college junior asks, "How can I get experience when everyone is asking for 'experience' before they'll give me a job?" Transferable skills in teamwork, leadership, and technology that were honed in high school and college will benefit any organization that is age-blind and talent-savvy.

What You Can Expect

Managing the Generation Mix is designed to help you understand the issue of age diversity in today's workplace so you can maximize the strengths of the age-diverse people with whom you work. It offers practical answers to questions that managers across the country ask every day:

- What is the "generation mix," and what has shaped each cohort's attitudes, values, and perspectives?

- How does generational history translate into everyday behaviors that often put age-diverse people on a collision course with one another?

- How do you bridge the understanding gap between generations to clear the obstacles to more productive relationships?

- How do you leverage everyone's unique talents so all team members focus on the only finish line that matters: the highest-quality results achieved in record time by the highest-quality talent?

- In addition to all the management skills you've already mastered, what other core competencies and best practices will help you more effectively lead a collaborative Gen Mix team?

Generational Issues Are Business Issues

The truth is, generational issues are important reflections of the critical business issues every organization is now experiencing as it transitions from the workplace of the past to that of the future. They are not merely a matter of "young versus old." Everyone, regardless of age, is now living through historic paradigm shifts in what a career is, what a working life is, and what today's unpredictable marketplace demands. How people react and respond to these changes often sets them on a collision course.

Your challenge as a Gen Mix manager, then, is to steer your multi-generational team members off the rigid course of "business as usual" into an open field of innovation, productivity, and learning. Your goal is to help everyone make that transition quickly, gracefully, and collaboratively. This book will help you reach that goal.

> **How generationally savvy are you?**
> **To find out, test your GENERATIONAL I.Q.**

Generational I.Q. Test: *Who Said It?*

Directions: Identify the generational source of each quotation below. Record your answers using these abbreviations:

S - Silent Generation   **X** - Generation X
B - Baby Boomer   **Y** - Generation Y

The answers are given at the end of the test.

____ 1. "I respect authority and follow the rules—but that authority has to earn my respect by being ethical and fair. Otherwise, I will do all I can do to circumvent the rules."

____ 2. "I don't take work for granted. Family is important and I need a balance. I am confident. Controlled leadership is important."

____ 3. "I wouldn't want [my managers] to be intimidating, but at the same time I want them to display that they have more knowledge than me. I want my bosses to respect me, but I also want to feel challenged by them. I don't want to feel like I'm on the same level as them. You want to look up to your bosses and feel that there is something you can learn from them. But at the same time, I want to be able to be comfortable around them."

____ 4. "The quality of my work is very important to me, and I want to be appreciated for that. I have other priorities besides my work; namely, family and faith. I prefer to work in a team environment. I need to feel that I'm making a difference in someone's life. I have a strong sense of loyalty to what I do and who I do it for." ➡

Generational I.Q. Test (cont.)

___ 5. "I'd rather be the authority than be subject to it."

___ 6. "Above all else, I want my life to make a positive differ-ence. I place a high value on learning—both academic and experiential. I am mistrustful of 'the System,' but expect government to play an active role in social services. Change is inevitable—it's both a challenge and a pleasure. Change is difficult but exciting."

___ 7. "When it's all said and done at retirement, I want to look back and be able to say that I was happy with my choices."

___ 8. "I still feel more comfortable with the hierarchy. But I want to be able to have input in decisions. I want my input to be considered."

___ 9. "I want lots of free rein in a creative, flexible, non-traditional environment and [to] be treated with utmost trust, or else forget it—I'm leaving to find security and recognition elsewhere."

___ 10. "Ideally I wouldn't have a boss, but someone who assigns projects and gives me free rein—some kind of guidance, especially when I am new to the job, but free rein to do as I see fit and as I think is best. I will be responsible for the consequences, but let me do my own thing with as little supervision as possible."

Answers: 1. B (age 44); 2. S (age 68); 3. Y (age 21); 4. B (age 48); 5. X (age 30); 6. B (age 57); 7. X (age 27); 8. S (age 58); 9. B (age 49); 10. Y (age 21).

What Is the Generation Mix?

WHAT SHAPES A GENERATION is infinitely complex. There are many superb studies and books that take an in-depth look at that complexity, detailing the historical circumstances that define members of every cohort. Here we offer a snapshot of the coming-of-age experiences that shaped the beliefs, attitudes, and perspectives of the four generations rubbing elbows at work.

The Silent Generation
(b. 1925–1942)

We've adopted Neil Howe and William Strauss's term "The Silent Generation" as convenient shorthand for the approximately 40 million Americans born in 1925 through 1942. The youngest Silents form the oldest cohort in the workplace today. We also acknowledge a group of "cuspers"—people born between 1943 and 1945—who may identify more readily with Silents' values than with Baby Boomers'.

Silents are "betweeners." Born too late to participate in the mettle-testing event of World War II and too early to become full-blown flower children, they found themselves stuck between "can do" Veterans and "I gotta be me" Boomers. Always one step out of sync with the times, Silents were young adults when it was hip to be teenagers. They were in their thirties when you couldn't trust anyone over thirty. They were in their forties when flower children proclaimed, "Make love, not war." Some experimented with free love—and found it wasn't so "free." (Divorce rates among their cohort began to soar in the 70s.) Some discovered mind-expanding drugs. ("[It was a time of] better living through chemistry," chuckles a 66-year-old.) Most embraced the *Ozzie-and-Harriet, Father-Knows-Best,* conformist, homogenized world of the 50s.

The more traditional Silents—"the Schwarzkopfs"—were awed by the sacrifices the "Greatest Generation" made to ensure a world "safe for democracy." They adopted their elders' values of loyalty, dedication, and commitment to command/control leadership in hierarchical organizations. They helped to rebuild the American economy in the 50s and looked forward to the ultimate rewards: status as an all-American family owning its own home, lifetime employment in a solid organization, and a comfortable retirement. They had their own war—Korea—but were lucky to suffer relatively few casualties.

The radical Silents—"the Steinems"—precipitated the social movements for which Boomers are often given credit. The first Students for a Democratic Society were Silents. The first Peace Corps volunteers were Silents. The major leaders of the Civil Rights and women's movements were Silents (Martin Luther King, Cesar Chavez, and Gloria Steinem).

While Silents still hold some of the most important positions in business and politics today, they have never had a U.S. President emerge from their ranks. Walter Mondale, Michael Dukakis, and Jack Kemp were passed over for Veterans (Ronald Reagan and George Bush, Sr.) or Boomers (Bill Clinton and George W. Bush). Playing the role of supporting cast (Jim Baker, John Sununu, Madeline Albright, Dick Cheney, and Colin Powell), they have been brilliant advisors, mediators, and aides. They are known more for their human relationship skills and their ability to negotiate than for their decisive leadership.

The Baby Boomers
(b. 1946–1960)

With cuspers at either end (1943–1945 and 1961–1964), this huge cohort of 76 million Americans has two distinct waves. Members of the "Woodstock Generation" were born in the 40s and early 50s. Even if they didn't attend that event or participate in the hippie counterculture, they shared the idealism and optimism of the late 60s and early 70s. For the second wave, those born in 1954 through the cusper year of 1965, we borrow the niche term "Generation Jones."

Many chroniclers of this cohort describe Baby Boomers as the original "Me Generation": the most spoiled, self-indulgent generation in U.S. history. These children of Veteran or Silent parents enjoyed a particularly child-focused upbringing in contrast to previous generations because there were so many of them. Consequently, unlike the Silent Generation, they were in the right historical place at the right time throughout their coming of age. They were kids when it was cool to be a kid, teens when it was cool to be a teen.

By the time the oldest Boomers reached college in the early 60s, they were ready to rebel against the safe, secure, "ticky-tacky" world their parents had created. Not content to live in "Pleasantville," where the parental imperative was "Get a good job and settle down," many set out not merely to define their individuality, but to create a more open, free society. As a 50-year-old fire chief put it, "We did not rebel just because we could. We wanted something better—more real."

By the time they emerged from three major assassinations (those of Veteran John Fitzgerald Kennedy and Silents Robert Kennedy and Martin Luther King), the

> ### *"Still Haven't Found What I'm Looking For"*
> #### — U2, 1987
>
> According to Jonathan Pontell, "jonesin" is slang
> for a strong craving for something or someone. "Our
> generation has the jones," he explains. "As children of
> the 60s . . . [we] were promised the moon. Then, in
> the 70s, as the nation's mood turned from hope to
> fear, we were abandoned. . . . Huge expectations left
> unfulfilled have deeply entrenched a jonesin' in us.
> This 'jonesin' has made us strikingly driven and
> persevering" (see www.generationjones.com).

Summer of Love, Kent State, and Vietnam, older Boomers had become the "over-thirties" they said they'd never trust. They cut their hair, donned business suits, and slipped into the very Establishment they had railed against the decade before. With their dreams of a social revolution shattered, many Boomers channeled their energies into their work and a dual search for material goods and spirituality as a way to affirm their self-worth.

Younger members of the Boomer cohort are now trying to establish themselves as another "in-between" generation. Too young to participate in more than the "feel" of Woodstock, Jonesers were nurtured on the high expectations of their idealistic Silent parents and Boomer siblings. However, they wound up reaping instead the high disappointments of the 70s. They learned early on that, of course, you couldn't trust politicians; that, of course, their elders' ideals didn't easily translate into action; that, of course, they would have to struggle to realize their dreams.

Considering themselves realistic idealists, Jonesers share the same defining characteristics of their older Boomer siblings: a child-centered upbringing, a focus on individuality and youth, and a distrust of anyone in authority. Only time will tell if they are truly distinctive enough to warrant their own name and identity.

Generation X
(b. 1965–1977)

We define Xers as the 52 million young adults born in 1965 through 1977. We also acknowledge a group of cuspers, born between 1960 and 1965, who identify more readily with Gen Xers than with Boomers. It wasn't until *Newsweek, Time,* and *BusinessWeek* popularized the term in 1993 that "X" became the official designation for this cohort. Most Xers hate it, but less so than the alternatives: Thirteeners (they are the thirteenth generation of Americans) or Baby Busters.

A generation of latchkey kids, Xers were born during one of the most blatantly anti-child phases in U.S. history.

Their Silent and Boomer parents had the highest divorce and abortion rates, highest number of dual-incomes, and most permissive parenting habits in our history. Viewed as intrusive obstacles to their parents' self-exploration, Xers found themselves in a faltering economy that plunged them into the highest child-poverty rates—and, later in their lives, the lowest wage and homeownership rates—since the Great Depression. In fact, they were the first generation of Americans to be told that they would not be as well off financially as their parents.

Having grown up in the aftermath of their parents' social rebellion, many Xers never developed strong connections to the traditional institutions (churches, schools, corporations, political parties) that had anchored their parents' coming of age. As a result, they became wary of institutions and learned early on that the only real security in a scary world lay within their own resourcefulness. And, indeed, during their formative years, the world was a terrifying place, even without a major war. Milk-carton kids became their MIAs. The AIDS epidemic put the lid on sexuality. Headlines screamed not of terrors abroad, but of those lurking down the street: Son of Sam, sexual abuse at home and in daycare centers, police brutality.

The most unsupervised generation of young Americans in our history, Xers were left to fend for themselves and developed a fierce "I can take care of myself" attitude.

They grew into independent, goal-oriented entrepreneur-ial thinkers whose ease with information and technol-ogy became one of their most important survival skills.

Then, in the late 80s, with college diplomas tucked un-der their arms, the oldest Gen Xers began to flow into a workplace that didn't want or need them. Their degrees earned them "McJobs"—low-skilled, low-paying posi-tions that undervalued their talents and contributions. The record downsizings of the early 90s confirmed what Xers knew all along: They had only themselves to de-pend on. Job security was an illusion; the only security lay within.

Ironically, that self-sufficient attitude, coupled with their techno-savvy and entrepreneurial impulse, has posi-tioned Xers as some of the most sought-after workers in the workplace today.

Generation Y
(b. 1978–1985)

In our book *Managing Generation Y,* we made the case that the time span between generations gets shorter and shorter as the pace of change accelerates. So unlike demographers who define Gen Y as the "Echo Boom," spanning more than 20 years (1980–2004), we prefer to talk about this cohort as the 29 million young adults born in 1978 through 1985.

Coming of age during the most expansive economy in the last 30 years, Gen Yers are the children of Baby Boomers and the optimistic, upbeat younger siblings of Gen Xers. The first true cohort of "Global Citizens," they have been told by parents, teachers, counselors, and religious leaders that they can make a difference in the world, and they have already started to prove it. The most socially conscious generation since the Steinems and Boomers, Yers are out in record numbers working for social causes from the environment to poverty, from local community programs to breast cancer research. In fact, according to the U.S. Department of Education, more than half of high school students did volunteer work during 1999, and according to UCLA, so did 75 percent of college freshmen.

Combine the altruistic impulse of Yers with their facility with technology, and you have a generation on fast-forward with self-esteem. When middle and high school students collaborate with teachers on how to use technology in the curriculum (thus shaping how and what they learn), when they easily create websites to share information on current projects, when they gain instant access to people and information around the world, it all adds up to a sense of empowerment that still baffles less techno-savvy adults.

Like Xers, Yers have also grown up in a scary world. In the 90s, terrorism became a national phenomenon with the Oklahoma City, World Trade Center, and Atlanta Summer Olympics bombings. School shootings in suburban and rural America exacerbated the fears urban Xers had always carried to class with them. Designer drugs, violence-packed video games, sexually charged advertising, TV, and movies bombarded their everyday lives and still do. However, while the media would have you believe these young adults are hopelessly derelict, the evidence points quite clearly to the contrary. Teen arrests, pregnancies, abortions, and drunk-driving accidents are actually down. Overall, Gen Yers are doing better than most adults realize or admit.

Influenced by education-minded Boomer parents, Gen Yers believe that education is the key to their success, and they're poised to be lifelong learners. Fueled by their facility with technology—a facility that makes even Xer skills look elementary—this "Digital Generation" is ready to learn anywhere, anytime. Add to that learning impulse Yers' ability to be great team players, and organizations are in for a challenge and a tremendous opportunity as this youngest cohort comes of age during the next five to 10 years.

Managing the Gen Mix

Each generation grew up in a very different world, with very different social conditions that helped define how they react and respond to life. Now, what happens when you encounter these cohorts in the workplace? What makes them distinctive and sets them apart from one another? What challenges can you expect as you try to shape them into a collaborative team?

Chapter 2.

Collision Ahead!
Your Gen Mix at Work

SCENARIO: It's Monday, 8:27 a.m. You've already answered 47 emails, run interference on a snafu in the shipping department, and scribbled some notes for your 8:30 a.m. team meeting. Dodging questions and requests, you sprint to the conference room, arriving just in time to hear Norm, a 63-year-old senior marketing manager, confront George, a 42-year-old sales manager.

"Hey, George," Norm asks impatiently, "where were you all weekend? I tried to get you on your cell phone and there was no answer."

"I told you, Norm," George says, "I turn my phone off on weekends. I don't want my time with my family interrupted."

"Well," the older man grunts, "I was able to get Jennifer, and it's lucky for you she had the answers I needed."

George shoots a glance—half-appreciative, half-concerned—at his 24-year-old assistant manager. For the past three months, he's been trying to wean Jennifer from her weekend attachment to her laptop and cell phone; obviously, it's not working. He knows that "technology addiction," fueled by a desire to make solid contributions, is already burning her out. She's highly enthusiastic but doesn't know how to pace herself.

Meanwhile, you get word that Michael, your 19-year-old IT supervisor, just called to say, "Start the meeting without me. I overslept. I'll be there in about an hour."

Unique individuals. Different generations. Colliding values, perspectives, and responses. No matter what age you are or which cohort you identify with, from time to time you will butt heads with one or more employees over what boils down to a generational misunderstanding. However, if you remember that these age-based clashes are mirrors of the business challenges every organization is facing in its transition to the workplace of the future, you'll have the inside track on addressing them more productively.

Silents in the Workplace

> *"I feel caught between an aggressive control generation and two consensus-belief generations. I over-identify who I am by what I do for work. I try to control how much work I bring home and how*

much family I bring to work. I try not to over-share at either end of my commute. As a first-generation divorcé and male single parent, I had no role models."

—56-year-old Silent cusper
Dean/HR Director, post-secondary education

Many Silents in the workforce today still wonder what happened to the loyalty, commitment, and "an honest day's work for an honest day's pay" ethic they inherited from the Veterans. They have a hard time understanding job hoppers. They're impatient with workers unwilling to make sacrifices for an organization. They're wary of those who rebel against the dues-paying and ladder-climbing paradigm they initially embraced.

Some Silents, though, have softened the more rigid Veteran management model of "When I say jump, you say, 'How high?'" Silent managers are more likely to make room for participation in problem solving and decision making than their elders were, and many Silent workers want to participate.

"I still feel more comfortable with the hierarchy," a 58-year-old office manager in the timber-products industry explains, "but I want to be able to have input in decisions and I want my input to be considered."

Silents are also more patient with mediating conflicts through "processing" and gathering opinions than their

❖ FOR YOUR INFORMATION ...

In 2001, most retirees were Silents. Those retiring at age 70 were born in 1931; those at age 65, in 1936; those at age 62, in 1939. By 2011, there will virtually be no members of this cohort left in the workplace.

"give me the bottom line fast" Gen X colleagues. This "process" versus "product" approach often causes conflict when, for example, they try to train Xers.

A sixtysomething told us, "Today younger people expect us to spout 'pearls of wisdom,' but they're impatient when we try to train them. I have to realize that they've 'gotten it' long before I think they have. They don't want the 'story'; they want to know the bottom line: How do you do it? Yet, sometimes I have to give them the background 'why' so they have the guiding principles to work from when I'm not around."

"Guiding principles," standardized policies, procedures, templates. Years of experience have taught Silents to rely on those tried and true ways of doing things, and many would still agree, "If it's not broken, don't fix it."

One challenge you face as a Gen Mix manager is to convince this cohort that the new standard in the twenty-first-century workplace is customization. The one-size-fits-all paradigm of solutions and strategies that worked so well in the past is gone. Customization of everything, from products and services to working arrangements, is in. And that requires more fluid, flexible policies and procedures as well as the willingness of everyone on the team to use their best judgment, day to day, moment to moment. Silents who have amassed years of experience have a broader context in which to make those judgments, but they need your support, encouragement, and recognition to do so. After years of working under command-and-control management, it will take time to convince them you are serious when you say, "Make the call," "Use your own judgment," and "I'll stand behind you—no matter what the outcome."

What Matters Most

When it comes to what matters about their jobs, Silents tell us that two things stand out: the work itself and the people they work with. But, unlike younger generations, they don't demand any "deep" meaning from their jobs. That was originally a Boomer imperative. Their work must be satisfying in and of itself, make a contribution to the organization, and reflect their skills and expertise.

Contrary to the stereotype that older workers don't want to learn new skills, many Silents certainly do. But unlike Xers or Yers, who want to amass marketable skills they can leverage elsewhere someday, Silents will learn new skills to be more effective and valued in their present jobs. They want to keep to contributing to the companies for which many of them have worked 20-plus years.

Studies have shown that the human mind doesn't slow down until after age 70. Therefore, patient trainers who are willing to teach "new tricks" to Silents in a "safe" environment, where the latter don't feel embarrassed or put on the spot, have great success. Conversely, savvy Gen Mix managers engage Silents in documenting and teaching the best practices they have mastered over the years to new hires to get those hires up to speed quickly. As Silents continue to retire every year, formalizing knowledge transfer becomes more imperative. Organizations can't afford to lose the experience and expertise of an entire generation.

A successful Silent high school teacher told us that the year before she retired "everyone seemed interested only in the ideas of new teachers. I had a lot to offer, but no one seemed to care." What a loss to young educators, who could have capitalized on 30 years of wisdom about classroom management and adolescent behavior: things that can't be learned from books or college courses.

The Silent cohort also wants to work with strong leaders who have proven track records. If you're a younger

Silent Free Agency

A 68-year-old retired nurse told us that her local hospital wouldn't accept her application to work part-time on a 7 p.m. to 11 p.m. shift.

"They told me I wouldn't get anything done in four hours," she sighed. "I told them, with my experience, I could do more in four hours than most of their staff could do in eight! But they wouldn't hire me."

"So what are you doing now?" we asked.

"Well," she perked up. "I work for several doctors' offices educating their senior patients about the proper use of medications. And, I advise real estate agents about 'senior-friendly' properties and how to make them attractive to older people. I charge an hourly rate."

"Then you're a free agent who owns your own business!"

"Well, I guess I am," she pondered, then smiled. "I guess I am."

manager, you're initially in a precarious position. You need to convince Silents that you have enough industry knowledge, self-confidence and people skills to deserve your leadership role, and that you need them as mentors whose wisdom and experience can shorten your own learning curve. A savvy Gen X manager quickly gained the support of a respected Silent staffer when she told him, "I bet you never dreamed you'd be working for someone young enough to be your daughter. But I've been appointed to this position and I'm going to do everything I can to help us all succeed. I'll need your experience and wisdom to help me do that. Can I count on you?"

Silents, with their strong work ethic, can be counted on. If you respectfully assert your authority and genuinely utilize their expertise, you will have success. Remember that they are great helpers and supporters and will be an integral part of your generation mix up until the moment they retire—and beyond.

A Final Note

We are already seeing industries scramble to rehire retired Silents as consultants, project leaders, or part-timers. For example, the healthcare industry, facing crisis-level nursing shortages, is exploring ways to recruit retired nurses as mentors without reducing their retirement benefits. The same holds true in education, where teacher shortages will reach crisis proportions within the next five years. Rather than writing off retired Silents, keep in touch with them. Update them on what's happening with their colleagues and with the organization. You may need them sooner than you think—in ways you can't imagine.

Boomers in the Workplace

"[Our generation had] the courage to challenge known stereotypes and the ability to see inequality. [We're] driven to the unknown, sensitive to other cultures, religions, and races, and have the spirit to care about others."

—A 51-year-old Veterinarian

During the downsizing daze of the late 80s to early 90s, disillusioned Boomers watched organizational hierarchies flatten, hundreds of thousands of jobs disappear, and the lifetime employment bubble burst. While some were strongly entrenched in secure positions, others were forced into the job-hopping mode Xers would see as "business as usual." A record number of them flatly rejected corporate America once and for all and set out to create their own businesses. Others stayed on board, struggling to do more with less, and championed teamwork and consensus as the way to meet their goals.

Boomers are understandably conflicted over the many changes in the workplace. Like Silents, they entered the workforce under one set of rules, and now, having climbed the ladder and paid their dues, they find themselves having to operate under another. In reaction, one group has dug in its heels, resisting the changes the new workplace demands. They perceive work only as "a constant necessity to survive" (a 52-year-old inventory manager) and "something [we] have to do" (a 46-year-old performance improvement manager).

Speaking for these "survivalists," a 51-year-old high school teacher describes himself and his Boomer colleagues as "the 'dinosaurs' in our department. We just trudge along following and enforcing the rules and regulations. Our out-of-school lives are quite limited. We put in the extra hours and give stability to the department. We're the first to arrive and the last to leave. We're cynical, yet we're the most loyal to the school."

Priding themselves on their ability to survive "sink or swim" management, these loyal, cynical "dinosaurs" complain about bosses who spend too much time with young hires and are angry about incentives and training opportunities they offer new staffers. "We're pampering Xers and Yers," complained a fortysomething in the banking industry. "They're a bunch of wimps."

Many Boomers, however, sound just like Xers and Yers when they proclaim they love work "as long as it's fun. As long as [we] can use our creativity" (a 44-year-old chiropractor). They are gracefully making the transition into the new global workplace, embracing the flexibility, techno-literacy, and entrepreneurial thinking it demands. They have learned the lesson Xers came of age with: Loyalty in the workplace begins with loyalty to yourself.

❖ FOR YOUR INFORMATION ...

Including cuspers, Boomers today are 37 to 58 years old. Jonesers (born between 1954 and 1965) are 37 to 46. In 2001, three million Boomers turned 55, with some eligible for early retirement. Many have bypassed the chance to retire, and a number have left their present positions to look for more flexible work arrangements. Eighty percent report they would be willing to work beyond age 65 if work conditions improve.

And that self-loyalty demands amassing new skills to stay valuable and creative in current positions—or to become more marketable for future opportunities. According to Tom Callahan, "more than 1.6 million [college students] are over 40, [and] nearly half of Americans aged 35 to 54 are taking adult-education classes" ("Go to School. AGAIN," *Parade Magazine,* Aug. 1, 2000).

These Boomers have also fallen into the free-agency mindset that Xers adopted as par for the course. "I take calls from headhunters all the time," admits a 44-year-old advertising director for a multimillion-dollar corporation. "I know I'm only a 'hired gun.' If my major account folds, I'm out of work, so it's important for me to know what's out there."

A 48-year-old VP of Human Resources for a large Midwestern bank adds: "I finally understood what Generation X was all about when the company I had worked with for 17 years merged and the new management downsized me. I knew then that I had to take care of myself. I have a good job now, but I don't know if I'll stay here until retirement. I'm looking for other opportunities."

Like many in his cohort, he's discovered that "empowerment," a buzzword Boomers embraced in the 90s, is all about taking responsibility for one's own career. Since downsizing is still a daily reality, with some organizations now "trading in" high-salaried Boomers for less expensive younger workers, free agency, self-loyalty, and self-responsibility will continue to be Boomer imperatives well into the next decade.

What Matters Most

Ask Boomers what's important to them at work, and you'll hear three things: respect, respect, respect. "It's not about money," a 44-year-old educator confides. "It's about respect. I don't go out and ask for it, but I work very hard to secure it."

Like Silents, Boomers have been around for decades. The oldest have been in the workforce since the early 60s, with an average job tenure of 15 years. They paid their dues in the old workplace and want to be recognized for their contributions in the new one.

A Sign of the Times

In March 2001, the AARP rolled out a new magazine, *My Generation,* targeting the growing wave of its newest members, Boomers.

Veteran and Silent subscribers to *Modern Maturity* have decidedly different issues than Boomers do, says editorial director, Hugh Delehanty, and they didn't want their publication to focus on Boomers and that cohort's "complex problems."

However, some managers, in their attempts to engage Xers and Yers, have overlooked the expertise of their Boomer employees. A 55-year-old elementary school teacher put it bluntly: "Our principal is falling all over Gen Yers, who I agree are sharp. But in the process, she's discounting Boomer teachers who have made this school great and who could serve as mentors to these young people. What she doesn't know is, Yers are going to leave for other opportunities because her leadership is so poor. They are all 'flash and dash.' We will still be here. And we are not happy."

No wonder Boomers are angry and resentful. Just when this cohort is reaching its professional prime, Xers and Yers are receiving all the attention. Accustomed to being in the right historical place at the right historical moment, the "Me Generation" is left shaking its head. They're not used to being out of the limelight, and they're not happy about being discounted.

As a Gen Mix manager, then, your challenge is to balance your enthusiasm for new young workers with genuine respect for the contributions of your Boomer staffers. How do you demonstrate that respect? Not surprisingly, Boomers have definite ideas about that. They want you to do the following:

- Honor their opinions, skills, knowledge, potential, and contributions.

- Offer them the flexibility and authority to try new ideas, and support them if they fail.

- Listen to them, individually and as a team, and genuinely factor their ideas into your decision-making process.

- Become a coach who facilitates, not dictates, and who challenges them to grow. Remember: Self-improvement is a major Boomer aspiration.

- Give them clear goals and guidelines along with the freedom and flexibility to do things their way.

- Offer constructive feedback, so they know what they're doing well and what they need to fix or improve upon.

Since Boomers will play significant roles on your Gen Mix team for the next five to 20 years, you can't afford to have them remain "not happy." Most have admirable track records and a strong work ethic; many are ready to become mentors to their younger colleagues. Unless they feel respected and recognized for their accomplishments, though, you will have little success getting them to work collaboratively.

Working for Balance

Fewer and fewer Boomers today are willing to keep up the frenetic pace that made them ideal foot soldiers in the 70s and 80s. Jonesers, in particular, are lobbying for family-friendly workplaces and work/life balance initiatives. They're supported by recent research that confirms that less "face time" at work has a positive impact on productivity. People who reduce work hours to spend more time with their families are actually more productive because they bring more energy and attention to their jobs. Getting eight hours of sleep each night, knowing you can work from home when your child or elderly parent is ill, and having the leeway to deal with personal issues all lend themselves to better results in less stressed-out work environments.

As organizations scramble to retain Xers and Yers, they need only look to talented, savvy Boomers for clues to what motivates talented people of all ages: challenging

Boomer Women Lead the Charge

Boomer women have had a profound impact on major workplace issues over the last 20 years. Lobbying for childcare, telecommuting, job-sharing, family leave, and flextime, they fought for the flexible staffing arrangements relevant to workers of all ages today.

They gave full rein to their entrepreneurial impulses when, in the late 80s and early 90s, institutional policies motivated them to leave staid corporations to open their own businesses in record numbers.

Presently these women lead most of the 9.1 million women-owned businesses in the United States, employing 27.5 million people and generating more than 3.6 trillion dollars in annual sales (National Foundation for Women Business Owners, Research Summary, May 11, 1999).

work for which they are respected, flexible working arrangements, coaching-style managers who offer opportunities for creativity and growth. How these are played out may vary from generation to generation, but these basic Boomer motivators resonate with everyone, regardless of age.

Generation X in the Workplace

"We are products of high divorce rates, the 80s Reagonomics era, and post-war parents. Every day we are making efforts [to create] well-being and a safe future by working on environmental issues, social acceptance, and lower crime rates."

—24-year-old Biological Technician in forestry

"What's all the commotion about?" Xers ask, scratching their heads. In the late 80s, when they first arrived in the workplace, things were already radically changing. They quickly learned that job security was a relic from the past. When "lean and mean" employers told workers of every age, "Go take care of yourselves; we're not responsible for you," Xers took that message to heart. They formed the first wave of free agents and went out to market their skills in ways that still leave their elders shaking their heads.

Initially typecast by older managers as disloyal, arrogant slackers with short attention spans who were unwilling to pay their dues, Gen Xers have emerged as the most sought-after workers in the marketplace. Their independent and entrepreneurial spirit, their facility with technology, and their adaptability and flexibility are exactly what the new workplace ordered—even if some older managers still don't see it that way.

❖ FOR YOUR INFORMATION...

Including cuspers born from 1960 to 1965, Xers are the 24- to 41-year-olds who make up one-third of the workforce. Out of their 52 million, nearly 18 million change full-time jobs annually. Although their average tenure on a job is three years, Xers are very likely to stay longer with organizations that tap into their creativity and entrepreneurial spirit by offering them ongoing opportunities to learn and add value.

Contrary to the slacker stereotype, Xers are extremely hard workers when focused and motivated. According to the U.S. Census Bureau, they work 3.6 percent more hours each week than the national average. In fact, one concern older managers have about their young colleagues is burnout. Xers (and Yers too, for that matter) who are still single and have few obligations outside work can easily get caught up in the 24-7 availability syndrome that some of their elders took for granted. Burnout is the inevitable result, both physically and mentally.

A fortysomething in the public-relations industry told us that her Gen Xers have a "connectivity addiction" problem. "They can't leave their cell phones, pagers, or laptops alone, even when they're on vacation," she said. "I see them burning themselves out too soon. I've learned to tell people when I'm on vacation, I'm unreachable. [Xers] find that hard to do."

What Matters Most

Today Gen Xers are understandably cautious as they navigate the unpredictable world of work. With an ironic skepticism some critics call cynical, they constantly test organizational waters: Are my talents being used? Am I learning new skills I can leverage wherever I go? Am I being recognized and rewarded for my contributions today, not five years from now? Do I receive the feedback I need to stay on track?

Xers know their security rests in staying on the cutting edge. "Jobs may come and jobs may go, but my career belongs to me" is the Xer anthem. (One that many Boomers echo.) Every organization needs knowledge workers who seize responsibility for their ongoing learning, and Xers are ready to do that.

Like people of any age, many Xers seek flexible work arrangements that facilitate work/life balance. Unlike Silents and older Boomers, who defined success by where they stood on someone's corporate ladder, Xers are more aligned with Jonesers, defining their success by their ability to create the life they want. And that life involves family, friends, hobbies, vacations—and the time to enjoy them.

Always in a hurry, Xers will often sidestep rules and procedures as they push for results. They're willing to take risks and innovate—even when it drives their older bosses crazy.

For example, not only do they want to participate in decision making like Silents and Boomers, they want instant access to the people making those decisions. Hierarchies and chains of command make no sense when they need information, resources, or answers fast. They're ready to run around any interference to get what they need.

Like Boomers, Xers also want challenging work. But for Xers (and Yers as well), you'll need to add something else to this universal motivator: increasing spheres of responsibility. Responsibility is the proving ground that you trust them, have confidence in them, and recognize their growth and development. In fact, for these cohorts, increasing responsibility is what makes them feel empowered. Deprived of that empowerment, they'll walk over to your competitor.

And herein lies the dilemma. Gen Xers consistently complain about the limited supply of "boxes" in most organizational structures: those up-line positions that traditionally have spelled responsibility, status, and salary increase. An articulate 26-year-old in the banking industry told a roomful of Boomer executives, "It's

"Dot Bomb" Provides Balance

In "Looking Beyond the Dot Bomb," journalist Karen Breslau interviewed a number of MBA students at Stanford's Graduate School of Business (*Newsweek,* April 30, 2001).

Surveying their reactions to the burst e-commerce bubble, she found some Gen Xers actually breathing a sigh of relief. Freed from frenetically writing business plans, these students could now enjoy their learning experience. They also said they would look for jobs that value quality of life over a workplace that was ultimately unsustainable.

like we're all stuck in a silo. I've been working here for three years now, and any movement up that silo is blocked by you Boomers. You're going to be around for quite a while, so what am I supposed to do? I'm ready to move now." The Boomers sat in stunned silence at the audacity of this young woman; the few Xers in the audience surreptitiously nodded their heads in agreement.

When options and opportunities for growth, mobility, challenge, and responsibility dry up, so does Xers' motivation. That young woman is thinking about her next career move, and if management doesn't do something quickly to retain her, she'll take her three years of training and experience to one of their competitors.

Old organization charts with their limited options for upward mobility can't contain—or retain—an energetic, ambitious young workforce. As a Gen Mix manager, here is one area you need to customize immediately. How can you create as many different career paths as there are talented employees?

The truth is, not everyone wants—or has the talent—to move upward into a management position. Gen Xers are often as willing to make lateral moves that keep them learning as they are desirous of vertical moves that demand more time-intensive commitments. What other options do you have at your disposal to recognize, reward, and develop young people who won't wait for five years, much less 15, to move through the silo?

Generation Y in the Workplace

"My boss is constantly asking for our feedback on what is working and what isn't, and she actually takes our advice. The environment is comfortable, as if she were an equal. She recognizes, when things don't go right, what the problem is and either tells us how to fix it or that it isn't in our hands to fix. She never blames everyone as a group and, most importantly, she is great at

*recognizing our accomplishments and hard work
individually [and] as a team."*

—20-year-old Student Volunteer

Consider this: The CEO of Wal-Mart sends his corporate
jet to a northeastern university to fly its top retail student
to Arkansas for a job interview.

More than 50 corporate recruiters scour the beaches of
Panama City, Florida, during Spring Break 2000 trying
to find the best talent among graduating seniors.

The career-opportunity section of a cutting-edge web-
site invites job prospects to take virtual tours through
offices, work areas, and the local community. "Here's
where you'll work. Here's where you'll live"—immediately addressing two major concerns of any job seeker.

Welcome to the competitive world of recruiting the new
kids on the block. It's all about speed, customization,
and interactivity: the communication qualities that appeal to the "Digital Generation." That means you will be
dealing with a cohort that is even more techno-savvy
and entrepreneurial than Generation X. Yers thrive on
challenging work and creative expression. They love
freedom and flexibility. They hate micromanagement.
And they are poised to be the most demanding generation in history.

What Matters Most

When we asked Yers what determines their choice of career, they told us that three things were essential:

- They want challenging, meaningful work that really impacts their world. Given their service impulse, that's no surprise. This expectation aligns them with members of older generations who have that same other-centered drive.

- They want to work side by side with committed coworkers. With their experiences in collaborative classrooms and on the playing field, Yers are much more poised to be great team players than more independent Xers or quarterback Boomers. Offer them the opportunity to work with enthusiastic, committed people, for collaboration is second nature to them.

- They want to reach their personal and financial goals—and some of those goals are lofty. For example, 70 percent of teens expect to work in professional jobs, earning very high salaries by the time they are 30.

Like workers of all ages, Yers claim that the relationship they have with their immediate boss is a critical factor in whether they stay on or leave a job. However, they are much savvier at an earlier age about what they want that relationship to be like.

❖ FOR YOUR INFORMATION ...

In 2001, the youngest Gen Yers were 16; the oldest 23. Twelve million are already in the workforce as full-timers, part-timers, or interns. Many will have had three to five part-time work experiences before they hit the workplace full-time. Yers will have a major impact on the workplace for every one of the next 10 years.

During an interview with a group of 16-year-old high school students, we asked: "What would you like us to tell managers about how you want to be managed?"

They responded: "We want them to understand we're still in school and need some flexibility in our schedules"; "We need them to be clear when they communicate what they want us to do. Don't leave without giving us answers to our questions"; "We want them to be patient with us. We're learning as we're going along."

Then a voice piped up and asked thoughtfully, "Don't they know we're the future workforce? Isn't it their job to make us want to come to work?"

There it is: The best managers create an environment where people "want to come to work." Management experts couldn't have said it better.

"The Next Great Generation"

The cover story in the July/August 2000 issue of
Modern Maturity proclaims: "Super kids! Here comes
the next Great Generation." Citing Howe and Strauss's
book *Millennials Rising*—and supporting our own
conclusions in *Managing Generation Y*—this article
aligns Gen Yers with their Veteran grandparents. As
the editors say in their introduction, "By and large,
these youngsters believe that hard work pays off, that
cooperation makes sense, and that good can, and
should, prevail."

For Yers, the key factor in that environment is how they
are personally treated by their boss. They consistently
tell us they have difficulty with older managers who
condescendingly correct them or even yell and scream.
Since they have enough rule-setters, micro-managers,
and stressed-out adults at home, Yers expect their relationship with adults at work to be more upbeat, helpful,
and mutually respectful.

Like members of older generations they have very clear
expectations of what they want from their Gen Mix managers. They want you to do the following:

- Spend time getting to know them and their
  capabilities.

- Establish a mentoring relationship with them.

- Focus on work, but be personable and have a sense of humor.

- Treat them as colleagues who are at work to add value.

- Be respectful and call forth respect in return.

- Consistently provide constructive feedback.

- Let them know when they've done a good job.

Don't Treat Us Like Kids

A 20-year-old college student in one of our workshops challenged a group of business executives, most of them Boomers.

"How many of you have kids at home?" he asked.

Most hands went up.

"Have you ever noticed how they try to hide from you? From your 'Do this, do that'?"

Smiles filled the room as heads nodded affirmatively.

"Don't treat us at work like you treat your kids at home," he continued with a twinkle in his eyes. "Lighten up. Don't be so serious. When it comes to giving us feedback, don't harp on what already happened, on what we did wrong. Tell us how to improve."

"Tell us how to improve." Confident, techno-savvy Gen Yers don't want overbearing parental figures at work. They want dedicated mentors and coaches who are willing to offer training in all kinds of skills that older generations take for granted or assume these young workers already know. Sure, they'll impress you with their dreams and aspirations, their goals and ambitions. But they are neither "sink or swim" Boomers nor sole-proprietor Xers. They need experts to give them direction, support their efforts, let them try to figure out some things on their own, and tell them how to improve.

Gen Yers are the most collaboration-ready members of your team. With the guidance of patient adults, this young cohort will want to come to work and be vibrant contributors to your Gen Mix.

Taking the Next Steps

This is your generation mix and some of the major challenges they pose. To get these cohorts to work collaboratively, two things are required:

1. You must bridge the understanding gap between generations to clear the air and remove the age-based prejudgments that hinder their working together. (We will cover this topic in Chapter 3.)

2. You must fine-tune your own management style so the needs of your multi-generational team members harmonize with the demands of an unpredictable, market-driven workplace. What core competencies must you master? What best practices must you implement to accomplish that? (We will cover this topic in Chapters 4 through 6.)

If you bridge the gap and fine-tune your skills, you will be well on your way toward creating a collaborative Gen Mix team.

Chapter 3.

Clear the Roadblocks:
A Gen-Mix Reality Check

LET'S FACE IT: Most people we complain about don't get out of bed in the morning mumbling, "Today I'm going to go to work and be difficult." (Okay, maybe a few do.) Rather, the difficulties we have with others—or pose to them—usually stem from colliding beliefs, values, assumptions, or expectations and/or our inability to communicate with others openly and honestly.

A Gen Mix manager, then, establishes a safe environment where workers of all ages can openly share who they are and what they bring to the table without fear of being judged, "fixed," or changed.

That bears repeating: "without fear of being judged, 'fixed,' or changed." People who value their own uniqueness are more likely to value their teammates' as well. Until they do, your attempts at creating a collaborative team will founder. Here are two of the most effective approaches we've discovered to move your team toward valuing their differences and focusing on their strengths:

1. Conducting a generational reality check

2. Exploring how each generation experiences workplace changes

1. Conducting a Generational Reality Check

Invite your team to an informal meeting to discuss generational diversity. Assure them that this is not a conflict-resolution session, but rather, an opportunity to share insights and understanding about age-related issues. The purpose is to clear up any misunderstandings that block more productive relationships. Create a comfortable environment, one that's conducive to fun. Provide refreshments and keep the tone light and engaging.

During the meeting, lead this brainstorming exercise:

❖ STEP 1

Break your team into smaller groups according to age cohorts:

- Generation Y—Born 1978 or later

- Generation X—Born 1965 to 1977

- Cuspers—Born 1960 to 1964 (Cuspers can join the group, Boomer or Gen X, they identify with.)

The Silent Perspective

Most Silents consistently perceive their strengths as loyalty, responsibility, altruism, and a strong work ethic.

"I have loyalty to my employer," explained a 59-year-old office manager in the timber-products industry. "My good work ethics set an example. I'm willing to learn new technology [since] I'm dedicated to doing the best I can in my job. I want to give the company their money's worth."

A 59-year-old supervisory physical therapist added, "I have allegiance to this country and its values as demonstrated in the workplace. I respect control leadership, my elders, and those who fought for my freedom. I believe we are responsible for our actions."

A 73-year-old psychologist proudly claimed, "We are hard-working, patriotic, and responsible."

- Baby Boomers—Born 1940 to 1960.
- Cuspers—Born 1943 to 1945 (Cuspers can join the group, Silent or Boomer, they identify with.)
- The Silent Generation—Born 1942 or before.

❖ STEP 2

Ask each group to select a facilitator and a note taker. The facilitator keeps the group on track and ensures

45

The Boomer Perspective

Boomers find their strengths in the social rebellion of the 60s and 70s. "We are cool!" said a 53-year-old municipal supervisor. "We made the current open society possible." "We challenged injustices," added a 49-year-old medical records keeper.

A 52-year-old administrator in a police department concurred: "We made a positive change. We questioned assumptions. We liberated society for the arts, movies, women, and people of color."

Like Silents, older Boomers are proud of their work ethic, though some admit their personal identity may be too closely wedded to their work. "I am what I do" is a Boomer anthem; work and self-worth are inextricably intertwined. In fact, a 51-year-old director of a health-care facility wondered about the "effect downsizing has on [the] self-worth and esteem" of his generation.

In reaction to the work addiction of their older siblings, Jonesers emphasize family values and a balanced life among their strengths. Leaving work at work and having interests outside their careers have become essential to their lifestyle—and they're proud of it.

A fortysomething job services representative put it this way: "The quality of my work is very important to me, and I want to be appreciated for that, but I have other priorities besides work, namely, my family and faith."

everyone gets equal airtime. The note taker records the major points of discussion.

The groups should focus brainstorming on these questions:

- What are some traits typical of your generation? (The note takers should record all the traits mentioned. Some traits will prompt discussion and debate, so instruct facilitators to let the discussion flow.)

- What are some traits typical of the other three generations? (Again, the note takers should record all the traits mentioned and the facilitators should allow discussion to flow.)

Each group should note traits for all four generations.

❖ STEP 3

Bring the entire team back together.

Explain to team members: *"The way others perceive us is often different from the way we perceive ourselves. Throughout our discussion we'll see how the same traits may be considered strengths by some and as weaknesses by others."*

Now ask each cohort group to report its results. Be sure to permit the flow of discussion. Also, make sure

The Gen X Perspective

Not surprisingly, Gen Xers heartily denounce their "slacker" stereotype. "We are not lazy!" proclaimed a 33-year-old employment director. They perceive themselves as hardworking, open-minded, and independent. They want to be productive, working smarter not harder, and have fun in the process.

Like younger Boomers, they value family as much as career. A 33-year-old workforce analyst summed up a common Xer theme when she said, "I value time off rather than more pay. I value flexibility in my work schedule because my family comes first."

They are also worried about the future of their children. A 28-year-old manager for an adult group home bluntly stated: "We're dedicated to parenting. We don't want our kids to be the 'shooters.'"

Like older Boomers, they care about issues like the environment, crime, and social equality. Like younger Boomers, they demand work/life balance.

that the reports proceed in an orderly fashion:

- Focus on Generation Y: Each group reports its list of traits for this cohort, with Yers going last.

- Focus on Generation X: Each group reports its list of traits for this cohort, with Xers going last.

The GenY Perspective

Many Yers describe themselves in cryptic terms such as "Generation X-treme," "The Cybergeneration," or "The Kids Who Think They Know What's Up." They're aware of the advantages their facility with technology gives them. "It takes us a little longer to figure out what we want," a 20-year-old software tester told us, "but we're more knowledgeable at an earlier age about things like money, politics, and news than other generations."

A 23-year-old retail clerk added, "I consider my generation responsible and caring. We're mature and are made aware at an early age of the perils facing us in the future. We take steps to avoid the less appealing futures and still know how to have a good time."

Then there was the 21-year-old salesperson in retail who brashly proclaimed: "We are cool people who are much smarter than our parents will ever be. Sometimes we don't use our common sense, but that's okay because we are still young."

- Focus on Baby Boomers: Each group reports its list of traits for this cohort, with Boomers going last.

- Focus on The Silent Generation: Each group reports its list of traits for this cohort, with Silents going last.

After the reports and discussion are completed, ask team members, *"What did we learn from this exercise?"* Emphasize this point: *Our task is to acknowledge and honor our differences and to focus on our strengths. We want to leverage both differences and strengths to maximize the learning, productivity, and innovation of our team.*

"Oh, So *That's* Why They're the Way They Are!"

Over the past three years in our Managing the Generation Mix workshops, we have engaged people in this reality-check process and gained important insights from the free-flowing discussions it stimulates. As cohorts listen to each other, they uncover the underlying reasons for their differences as well as the commonalities that unite them. Both facilitate more productive relationships.

Authority Issues

Most Silents are still very respectful of titles and the people who hold them. Boomers, on the other hand, pay lip service to, but are generally suspicious of, anyone in authority. Most Xers and Yers say they respect a person in authority if he or she has the credibility to back it. They want bosses who are knowledgeable not only about their own jobs but about those they're managing. For young workers credibility means "You know what I'm up against. You know the challenges and stresses in this job because you've been there. And you're here to help me succeed as easily and quickly as possible."

Work Ethic

Older generations hear firsthand why Xers and Yers don't embrace the same "pay your dues" work ethic they do. When young employees talk about absentee parents who missed key events during their growing-up years, the message comes across loud and clear: "We don't want to do the same thing to our kids. Don't worry. We'll get the work done. Give us the flexibility to take care of our lives outside of work, and we'll bring more attention and energy to work."

Conflicting Management Expectations

Underlying the work-ethic discussion is a basic conflict between management approaches: the old paradigm of "face time" management (employees must be onsite during specific hours) and the new paradigm of "results" management (get the work done wherever, whenever, as long at you meet or beat standards and deadlines).

A Gen X HR recruiter confided that she would willingly give up two thousand dollars of her pay a year to work from home two days a week. "A majority of my tasks can be done from home on my PC, any time of day or night" she explained. "I wish I had the flexibility to determine when I accomplish those tasks without having someone breathing down my neck, enforcing a set schedule."

A Silent manager in a state consumer agency added that she's been doing "results management" for over a decade. "I don't understand why other managers don't 'get it,'" she said. "I get more productivity from my team when I allow them to pace themselves." Another Silent concurred: "I just told a young staffer he could have an extra hour to go to lunch with his wife today. I know he'll get his work done and family is very important to him."

Patience Versus Speed

It's beneficial for impatient Xers and Yers, who want everything *now,* to understand the value of Silents' problem-solving skills and Boomers' devotion to consensus. Slowing things down so everyone has the opportunity for input and ownership has become redefined as a wise investment rather than a waste of time. Even a Gen X manager who complained about the Boomers on his staff—"They're so slow! They want to process everything, and I want to get to the bottom line"—finally admitted, "I guess I need to be more patient."

Two-Way Mentoring

Xers and Yers liven up when groups discuss mentoring: "If you coach me on negotiation strategies," said a Gen Xer to a Silent, "I'll teach you the latest Internet tricks."

A fortysomething astrophysicist at a world-class research facility explained: "I would not have become a successful scientist without the guidance and support of many wonderful mentors along the way. So being a mentor is the best way I can think of to pass on that precious gift of opportunity to the next generation and return the favor of those that helped me."

Rather than hoarding his invaluable experience or adopting the counterproductive "I had to walk five miles in the snow, so should you" attitude, this Boomer exemplifies the cross-generational partnering necessary for successful collaboration.

Everywhere we go, managers tell us the median age in their business is getting older and older, and they're concerned about finding the next generation of leaders. Yet, when we ask them, "What are you doing to groom young employees for leadership positions?," they look at us sheepishly. "Well, we really don't have a mentoring program yet." You can't afford not to have one *right now*.

Common Ground

Collaboration becomes easier when different generations identify not just what separates them but also what unites them. Your Gen Mix team will find that under the strata of diversity lies a bedrock of unifying needs and expectations. For example, a fiftysomething insurance agent was amazed to learn that younger employees want the same things that he does: creative challenges, the opportunity to add value, increasing responsibility, and flexibility in scheduling. The only difference, he realized, is that they want, expect, and demand these at the beginning of their careers. Finally, toward the end of his career, he's acknowledging that such things matter to him—and that he can have them.

Or take the issue of how people want to be managed. Each generation looks for the same thing: respectful managers who give them clear directions balanced with the freedom to do the work their own way. They want team leaders who are democratic rather than autocratic, who are coaches rather than "bosses."

Everyone—regardless of age—says that their relationship with their immediate manager is one of the most important factors in their decision to stay with or leave an organization.

2. Exploring How Each Generation Experiences Workplace Changes

Once people begin to see their differences as well as their common ground and are able to focus on their strengths, engage them in one or both of the following discussions.

❖ DISCUSSION ONE

Let's talk about the changes in today's workplace. What were your expectations about a career and a working life when you first entered the workplace? How have they changed? How are *you* experiencing the changes in the workplace now?

During the discussion of changes in the workplace, emphasize this point: *Since we're all living during this fast-paced, often unpredictable moment in history, no one generation has a monopoly on defining the new workplace—not Silents or Boomers who hold top positions; not Xers or Yers with all their techno-savvy and free-agency attitudes. Rather, our workplace is defined by a market-driven, fiercely competitive economy. All of us, regardless of age, need to be flexible, techno-savvy, entrepreneurial knowledge-workers. All of us must be lifelong learners, sharpening our skills and leveraging our talents to get the best work done every day.*

FYI: The Facts

All these cohorts are now driving through today's fast-paced business terrain, but it sure looks different from each lane. Silents typically experience these changes—globalization, technology, downsizing, restructuring, and reengineering—as revolutionary; everything about work is changing. For Gen X and Gen Y the changes are exciting. Every change is an opportunity they want to seize and turn into their own personal proving ground. The Boomer majority in the middle tends to feel the most conflicted about the new workplace.

❖ DISCUSSION TWO

What do you feel you have to offer that will be particularly valuable to those of other generations on our team? How can *you* benefit from the differences of those in other generations?

Re-emphasize this point: *If we are going to create a collaborative team that gets the best work done every day, our task is to maximize the contributions each person on this team makes. We respect and honor our differences and approach them not as a reason for conflict but as springboards to learning, productivity, and innovation.*

FYI: The Facts

Each generation can benefit from the different perspectives and strengths of the others. Silents usually have the most experience, the best institutional memory, and the highest degree of wisdom. Gen Xers and Yers bring fresh ideas and energy to the mix. Boomers bridge the gap between the past and the future; they tend to relate to both the perspective of the most experienced people and the entrepreneurial impulse of the youngest in the mix.

The Next Step

Your team's discussion of generational issues will be an eye-opener. It isn't the panacea for all future misunderstandings, but it will begin to clear the air. However, helping people understand their differences and unique strengths is only the beginning. If you stop here, you're left with "Now that we understand one another, let's be polite and make nice." That works—as it does for all diversity issues—but only to a point.

The next step is to steer your team toward the finish line: the highest-quality results achieved collaboratively in record time by the best people. Age is no longer an issue; the willingness and ability of each team member to leverage their strengths and their contributions is.

The best Gen Mix managers maximize each member's productivity by mastering three core competencies: *focus, communication,* and *customization.* They focus members on the team's mission and goals as well as the roles they will play to accomplish them. They create easy-to-use communications systems that provide information and resources *just-in-time,* all the time. And they keep their people energized and engaged by customizing incentives to fit the diverse needs of an age-diverse team.

Chapter 4.

Focus: It's All About the Work

THINK ABOUT IT: The reason why you hire people in the first place is to get the best work done every day. Work is all about "the work." The work itself can be the most powerful common ground when it's meaningful, challenging, and varied, when it offers everyone opportunities for growth, learning, recognition, and reward. Remember, Silents claim that work motivates them when it's satisfying; Boomers derive their identity from it and want to be respected for it; Xers find their security in amassing skills from it; Yers want to make a difference through it.

Your job is to ensure that everyone understands that working together to get lots of great work done is not negotiable. It's what everybody is expected to do together every day. The first core competency of the best Gen Mix managers, then, is *focus:* keeping people of all ages on track and in harmony with the mission, goals, roles, and responsibilities inherent in the work.

This chapter provides you with seven "best practices" for establishing and maintaining focus. Practices 1 to 5 are essential focusing steps and should be done in the order we describe. Practices 6 and 7 can be done at your discretion when the team is ready to move to a higher level of collaboration.

The Essential Focusing Steps

BEST PRACTICE 1: Re-ignite Your Team

Why Are We Here?

The classic complaint that employees of all ages have about managers is "We don't know why we're doing what we're doing. And we certainly don't know where our roles and responsibilities begin and end."

Get rid of these complaints immediately by making the mission of your organization and your team the compelling answer to "Why are we here?" According to our colleague Dick Barnett, author of *Re-Ignite Your Business: The Secret of Leading with Confidence, Ease, and Certainty,* 95 percent of CEOs haven't a clue why their companies exist. That's discouraging.

Vision is about the future, but mission is all about right now. If your organization has a mission statement, when was the last time you pulled it out, dusted it off, and engaged people in a lively discussion about the purpose and values that drive the work they do right now? If your organization doesn't have a mission statement—or if it's so old as to be meaningless—seize the opportunity to create one collaboratively.

Re-igniting Your Team

Focus on your organization's mission. Ask your team to discuss the following questions; then use their answers to re-ignite their commitment.

- Is our organization's mission still compelling enough to motivate us to contribute our best? If not, why not? What would it take to make us willing to contribute our talents every day?

- Has the mission dramatically changed over time? Does it need revision to get us in sync with marketplace realities?

- How can we redefine the mission so we can really buy into it?

- Are we aligned with its values? If not, why not? What would it take to achieve alignment?

BEST PRACTICE 2: Define Your Team/Project Mission

Missions Within the Mission

Each team, each project, each committee also has its own mission. Every time people begin working together as a group, invite them to define why their group exists and how its purpose aligns with the organization's. Their tasks—setting goals, handling conflicts, making decisions, allocating resources—are set within a broader context. Thus, it is important for them to ask: How will this further our team's (or project's, or committee's) mission? How does this support our organization's mission?

Defining Your Team/Project Mission

Ask team members to participate in a brainstorming session to clarify their present mission or that of their next project. Use the following questions as guidelines, and work toward consensus.

- Why does our team/project exist?

- What do we do that no one else can do? What will the project accomplish?

- What makes our team/project special?

- What would the organization lose if our team/ project disappeared?

Once the team has defined its mission, ensure that each member has a copy of the mission statement and that a copy is posted where everyone on the team can see it.

Don't underestimate the power of "pride of affiliation": the bragging rights that come along with being part of a great team that has a great mission with a great track record doing great work with great people.

BEST PRACTICE 3: Clarify the Team's Work

What's the Work?

Once the team has defined its mission, the focus turns to the work. The team now must clarify such things as its goals, tasks, deadlines, and guidelines.

Clarifying the Team's Work

❖ STEP 1

Facilitate your team's discussion of these important questions:

- What work needs to be done by this team (or on this project)?

- What tasks and responsibilities must be accomplished?

- For each project, task, and responsibility, what are the major goals and deadlines?

- What are the key guidelines that must be observed?

- How will success be measured?

Focus on the guidelines that are truly necessary, not just on the ones that have always existed. Re-evaluate

The Scope of Our Work

Projects, Tasks, and Responsibilities	Goals and Deadlines	Guidelines	Is Guideline Negotiable?

each one to identify which are negotiable and which are not. (See worksheet "The Scope of Our Work.")

❖ STEP 2

Once everyone is clear about the team's work, decide who will continue as a member and who will not. Those unable or unwilling to commit themselves to team accountabilities cannot continue as members. They may be more effective on another team or in another department; they may need more training or outplacement counseling. Every player on your team must be assured that he or she is working with committed, enthusiastic contributors. We've discovered that when everyone knows others are willing to add value, contribute 100 percent, and pull their weight to get the best work done, most conflicts dissipate.

❖ STEP 3

Before a project begins, ask team members to discuss how progress will be benchmarked and how success will be defined. How will they measure individual contributions as well as those of the team as a whole? How much "tolerance for mistakes" will the team allow in order to reach the best solutions? How much time for "trial and error" must be factored into deadlines?

To stay ahead of your competition, your team must be willing to innovate and take risks. Consequently, old methods of measuring success may not work at all in today's unpredictable marketplace, and may even be counterproductive. We've discovered that the people doing the work often have the best insight into how to evaluate their work.

BEST PRACTICE 4: Define Each Team Member's Mission

Who's on First?

Once you know who's remaining on your team, clarify each member's personal mission: his or her role or function on the team. Few things destroy a team faster than a manager not helping players define their roles or players not understanding those roles.

Defining Each Member's Mission

Ask your team to answer these questions:

- What resources of time, energy, skills, knowledge, and talents will each person contribute to the team effort?

- How will we collaborate to get the work done?

- Who is best suited to do what? By when?

- How flexible is each team player in terms of learning new skills, implementing new strategies, and changing direction when necessary?

- What starring roles and what supporting roles is each person willing to play?

Successful sports franchises demand individual excellence, no matter what role an athlete plays. When called upon, a bench player needs to contribute 100 percent as readily as a starter. In fact, the most successful teams have "deep" benches as well as stars who can assist as well as score, who can follow as well as lead. Team members who can successfully function in a variety of roles become your most valuable "utility" players, offering the team the flexibility it needs to seize new opportunities or to change strategies quickly.

BEST PRACTICE 5: Leverage Uniqueness

Immediately help team members clear the air so they have the best shot of proceeding quickly and collaboratively with the work. Try a round-table approach in which each member is given equal time to share his or her views on these three issues:

- The talents, skills, knowledge, and experience that he or she brings to the team

- Areas where personal performance improvement is possible within the next month (or quarter)

- What kind of support the member would like, in terms of coaching, training, or mentoring, in order to make the improvements

For each member, the team should do the following:

- Affirm the member's strengths by offering specific examples of how he or she has used those strengths to further the team's mission and goals.

- Offer suggestions for how they can help the member improve performance. Who on the team (or elsewhere, for that matter) can serve as a coach to get this player up to speed more quickly?

Return to this discussion periodically to update everyone on the performance improvements. Many conflicts will also disappear when everyone realizes their coworkers are committed to becoming more and more valuable team players.

Moving to a Higher Level of Collaboration

BEST PRACTICE 6: Create Learn/Teach Plans

Another approach to leveraging strengths is having team members share the three to five things they want to learn and to teach over the next three months. Support every opportunity you can find to facilitate two-way mentoring and coaching. For example, match the seasoned employee who's an expert customer-service rep with a new hire who needs those skills fast. How can the expert shorten the learning curve for that person? In turn, what new insights and ways of doing things can new employees offer the team?

A 27-year-old finance supervisor in public education said of her generation, "We have a willingness to learn, but also a desire to teach." Everyone on your team must be poised to be lifelong learners and lifelong teachers. In fact, offer more formal training in teaching and facilitation skills to those who have the talent and desire.

BEST PRACTICE 7: Banish Job Descriptions

If you really want to energize your team, throw away job descriptions and start from square one by dividing up tasks and responsibilities. Now that members know the team's mission and goals, as well as all the work that must be done, ask them to divvy up assignments based on each one's talents and preferences.

Ask them to discuss these three issues:

- What work they would love to spend more of their time doing

- What talents they are presently not using that would benefit the team

- What tasks and responsibilities they are not presently accountable for that would maximize their individual strengths

---

A Case in Point

A 62-year-old who recently retired from a government position was a visionary. Eight years ago, after being promoted to management, she met with her people to find out how they wanted to use their talents and skills every day. They decided to ditch their job descriptions and redefine how to invest their time. The result? Three years of exceptionally high productivity and morale.

Upper-level managers finally put an end to the "experiment" because they couldn't stand the freewheeling style of this upbeat department. Forced to return to the old "ball and chain" ways of doing things, the team lost its enthusiasm as well as its innovative manager.

The lesson? Putting people into, and keeping them in, a prefab box on an organization chart is an ineffective way to leverage their talents.

Author and management consultant Theodore Zeldin claims that most people only use 20 to 25 percent of their potential in their present jobs. Maximize that potential by giving everyone first dibs on doing the work they love to do. Then, divide up the necessary but less glamorous tasks.

The evidence is clear: When people spend most of their day doing what they love to do, great performance skyrockets. This process also gives everyone the chance to reevaluate "the work": What routine tasks can be automated, streamlined, or outsourced so people can capitalize on their talents and avoid wasting time on boring work?

Focus your team on their mission, goals, roles and strengths. Then, let them get on with the work.

❖ **Review ...**

BEST PRACTICES

1. *Re-ignite your team.*
2. *Define your team/project mission.*
3. *Clarify the team's work.*
4. *Define each team member's mission.*
5. *Leverage uniqueness.*
6. *Create learn/teach plans.*
7. *Banish job descriptions.*

Chapter 5.

Communicate Just-in-Time, All the Time

A THIRTYSOMETHING hit the bull's eye when she said, "In an increasingly hectic environment, managers are communicating less with their peers and direct reports. This poses a challenge to successfully getting one's job accomplished. I have learned how and when to approach management in hectic situations and communicate effectively to get what I need in a very short period of time."

Why not proactively confront the challenge of effective communication so everyone can work successfully? You can do it by:

- Creating the expectation that even in a hectic environment, communication on all projects, assignments, and important issues will be done *just-in-time, all the time*

- Helping teams create easy-to-use communication systems that facilitate good communication

We found expert Gen Mix managers across the nation doing just that. Fourteen of their best practices are presented here. We've numbered them as additions to the seven best practices provided in Chapter 4.

Best Practices: Communication

BEST PRACTICE 8: Seize Informal Timeout Times

Anyone who has children knows that the most important family discussions often occur in the car on the way to the grocery store or while you're making dinner, stacking the dishwasher, or tinkering with the lawn mower. Somehow informality facilitates significant sharing.

The same is true in the workplace. Many young workers tell us they appreciate informal opportunities to get out of the office to talk with their managers about their work, dreams, capabilities, and outside interests. Be as creative as you can. For example, Bruce frequently takes staff members on long walks around his New Haven neighborhood to catch up, coach, and brainstorm.

A Gen X senior partner in a prestigious financial consultancy told us, "My boss loves going out to lunch, so I make a point of scheduling time to meet with him at his favorite restaurant. He has to eat, so this is my best time with him."

Go for a walk, have coffee, go out to lunch—anything that works for you and your young employees. You'll learn more about them during these informal times than in formal settings.

BEST PRACTICE 9: Establish Formal Timeout Times

Having said that, it's also important to schedule one-on-one sessions on a consistent basis, daily or weekly depending on individual needs. Most Silents and Boomers are used to this approach and prefer to capture your undivided attention in a more formal setting.

Create an easy-to-use agenda to guide your one-on-one discussions (see example, next page). If both you and your employee come prepared, you can minimize time spent on defining problems and maximize time spent on solutions and commitments. Also, to avoid confusion or misunderstanding, be sure that both of you document the discussion and commitments.

BEST PRACTICE 10: Circulate Everyone's To-Do Lists

Ask team members to make to-do lists outlining their team commitments, and to email them to everyone working on a specific assignment or project. This can be done on a daily or weekly basis. The message is "This

— Agenda —
Manager/Team Member Meeting

Manager: _____ Team Member: _____

Date: _____

Work in Progress:

Problems/Questions:

Resources Required:

Commitments Made:

Signed:

_____   _____

         Manager   Team Member

is what I'm working on today/this week. These are the deadlines and results I'm committing to."

The popularity of "mastermind" groups confirms that people are more productive when they share their commitments. Procrastination becomes more difficult when "saving face" in front of peers is a motivator.

BEST PRACTICE 11: Publicize Weekly Accomplishments

Send out brief weekly reports that let others know "This is what I accomplished this week." Such reports not only keep people apprised of the work in progress, but also motivate them. Personal success breeds more success; individual accomplishments inspire and energize others.

BEST PRACTICE 12: Create Unique Email Subject Lines

For team communications, create unique subject lines to tip off coworkers that this email refers to a project at hand and must be read immediately. With their own "Code Blue," members can scan through email files quickly for those that directly pertain to them.

Set a standard for how often emails should be checked at work; also set one for response-turnaround times. Having such standards is especially crucial during crunch times, when deadlines approach, resources are required, and questions need answers. Members need to know that their communications are being read and will be answered *just-in-time*.

BEST PRACTICE 13: Encourage Members to Ask for Help

Make sure members know that whenever they, as individuals, find themselves stuck, off track, or out of focus, they should immediately ask for help. While some may regard this as a show of weakness, it is the most intelligent approach to getting things done. Recognize people who know where to go and to whom to go for resources, answers, or advice.

Consider using an "Asking for What I Need" form when your people don't have immediate access to you or to one another (see form, next page). The requester has the responsibility to suggest how others can deliver on the request. That might mean anything from providing a training opportunity or holding an impromptu team meeting to granting more results-delivery time or doing more in-depth research on a topic. The requester also has the responsibility to indicate deadlines and who will conduct follow-up.

The recipient has the option to deliver the request as stated or to make appropriate revisions.

— Form —
"Asking for What I Need"

To: _____ Date: _____

From: _____

Subject: I need your help!

Request:

Suggestions for delivering on request:

Expected date for accomplishment: _____

Follow-up conducted by: _____ Date: _____

RESPONSE TO REQUEST:

- ☐ Accepted as requested.
- ☐ Needs some revision. Let's talk.
- ☐ Hold until this date _____ because:
- ☐ I can't do this now because:

BEST PRACTICE 14: Create an Experts Database

Facilitate your team's just-in-time access to "the best in the business" by creating an experts database. List names, areas of expertise, and experience (including projects successfully completed, innovations introduced or implemented, customers served, and contact information). In addition to acting as a valuable networking resource, this database advertises the accomplishments of the key contributors in your organization.

BEST PRACTICE 15: Create a Shared-Notes System

If your organization takes a team approach to dealing with customers or clients, it's imperative to have a communication system that records "interaction history."

For example, each year RainmakerThinking deals with hundreds of organizations, meeting planners, association directors, and speakers' bureaus. Because several staffers are involved with delivering our products and services, each one keeps documentation on the salient points of our communications with customers, including telephone conversations, email, and snail mail. This information is consistently shared with appropriate team members so everyone is up to speed. Consequently, any member can step in at a moment's notice, fully prepared to continue business without customers having to repeat information or to explain previous agreements. Staffers feel prepared and professional; customers are impressed with the just-in-time service they receive.

BEST PRACTICE 16: Hit the Ground Running With Action-Packed Meetings

Most business meetings are colossal wastes of time. Everyone knows that; few are courageous enough to stop the waste. For example, managers in one large governmental agency spend up to 80 percent of their time in meetings. They all agree that most sessions are merely ego shows and power plays, but no one dares to eliminate them.

Get out of the meeting trap with these guidelines:

- Don't meet just for the sake of meeting. Meet only when you have a compelling reason to pull people away from their work and can justify the cost of their hourly rate. If the only reason for meeting is to convey information that can be delivered via email, reports, or memos, you are wasting valuable time.

- Ensure that the meeting's purpose is clear to everyone by defining that purpose in your pre-meeting announcement and again at the start of the session itself.

- Save time during meetings by assigning "home-work" beforehand. What do people need to read, think about, bring with them, or come prepared to discuss so the meeting will be more productive?

- Determine beforehand who *really* needs to attend a particular session. Invite everyone on the team, but when it's not a command performance, let those who don't have to be there off the hook. The message is "Feel free to come to this meeting if you are interested and want to offer your input. However, if you are engaged in more pressing work, feel free to pass."

- Most meetings end in too much talk and too little action because of confusion between what was discussed and what was decided upon. The remedy? Give everyone a discussion/decision form to fill out as the meeting progresses (see form on next page).

  Each person will thus walk away with a clear picture of what was left at the discussion level and what actions, accountabilities, and deadlines were agreed upon. No one will have to wait for a meeting-minutes version of documentation. In fact, the discussion/decision form can easily substitute for formal minutes.

Discussion/Decision Form

Issue	Discussion/Decision (Mark decisions w/asterisks)	Date to Be Effected	Key Person(s) Involved	Review Date	Completion Date

- Give those who want it the chance to learn basic facilitation skills; then rotate the leadership of your meeting. You can sit back, observe, and offer the leader feedback on his or her effectiveness. Remember, running a meeting is a key skill for anyone who aspires to management.

- Ensure that all your meeting facilitators practice "balance of participation." That means they encourage everyone to contribute to a topic before the floor is open for general discussion. It's important to make sure that quieter members who have valuable things to say get equal airtime, especially if your team has some articulate heavy hitters.

- End each meeting with a quick evaluation. Ask people: "On a scale of one to 10, with 10 being the highest, how would you rate this meeting? What would it take to make our next meeting a '10'?" Have someone record and distribute the suggestions. Be ready to implement the best in time for the next meeting.

BEST PRACTICE 17: Evaluate Team Effectiveness

For many people, young or old, becoming a great team player requires learning new skills. Periodically gather together your members to evaluate how well they're working as a team. Ask them to discuss the following questions:

- What are we doing together that's working well?

- What are we doing that's not working well enough?

- What do we need to do to be more effective?

- Who's accountable for the change, and by when?

Decide what training or coaching they need as a team to improve their collaborative efforts.

BEST PRACTICE 18: Evaluate the Effectiveness of Individual Team Members

Determine how well each team member is doing right now in light of your standards for successful team playership. (Feel free to customize standards to make this evaluation even more meaningful to your situation.) Keep the standards in the forefront of everyone's mind by periodically asking members to do a self-evaluation. Use their responses as a topic in your next one-on-one meeting. Recognize successes and set up coaching opportunities for improvement.

The Team Playership Rating Evaluation (see next page) will help you put this best practice into use in your organization.

— Evaluation —
Team Playership Rating

Directions: Using the scale below, rate yourself on the qualities of effective team playership. At our next one-on-one meeting, be prepared to discuss your strengths and one or two areas you want to work on during the next quarter. Bring suggestions for how I can help you improve.

RANGE OF SCALE

1 = Ineffective   5 = Moderately effective
10 = Highly effective

The willingness and ability to ...

1. Work interdependently   1 . . . . 5 10

2. Communicate openly and honestly   1 . . . . 5 10

3. Contribute the best of my talents, knowledge, skills, and experience   1 . . . . 5 10

4. Take risks and be innovative   1 . . . . 5 10

5. Focus on problems rather than personalities   1 . . . . 5 10

6. See and honor diverse perspectives   1 . . . . 5 10

7. Take 100 percent responsibility for my roles and goals on the team   1 . . . . 5 10

8. Behave and speak in ways that move others toward me or at least no further away from me   1 . . . . 5 10

➡

Evaluation (cont.)

9. Eliminate put-downs, fault-finding,
   or blaming from my relationships
   with coworkers   1 . . . . 5 10

10. Build trust, foster collaboration, and
    support each member's personal
    development and achievements   1 . . . . 5 10

Suggestions for improvement:

BEST PRACTICE 19: Help Teams Create
Conflict-Resolution Guidelines

One of the most difficult skills for teams to learn is how
to handle conflicts with one another *just-in-time*. You
can refocus them on their mission, goals, and work, but
sometimes personalities will still clash. That's human.
Since it's counterproductive to have staffers run to you
over run-ins with others, help them establish guidelines
to get themselves back on track quickly. What principles
and guidelines will they follow so conflicts are resolved
quickly and respectfully?

A retired Silent from the U.S. Forest Service told us that, late in his career, one of his managers helped his team answer that question; then the agreed-upon guidelines were printed on card stock and distributed to everyone. Whenever he had a conflict with someone, he'd pull the card out of his wallet and re-read the guidelines. "It worked," he smiled. "It was pretty hard to continue fighting when we both knew what we had committed to."

A 40-year-old VP of Media at a prestigious PR firm added that her team members habitually ran to her with their complaints about one another. After asking the obvious question so frequently—"Have you talked this over with so-and-so yet?"—she threw the conflict issue back in their laps. "They know now that their first step is to resolve the issue themselves. The second step is for both of them to come to me. Not one, but both. Interestingly, I'm not a referee much any more."

Use the Communication Credo (see next page) as a springboard to create conflict-resolution guidelines. Print guidelines on card stock and encourage your team to follow the principles and process when conflicts arise.

BEST PRACTICE 20: Call an Innovation Summit Quarterly or Biannually

This is an enjoyable, high-energy, high-visibility event that sparks creativity and entrepreneurial spirit. The

Our Team's Communication Credo

❖ We believe in mutual respect, open communication, and the willingness to listen to each other.

❖ We support the principle that we can respectfully agree to disagree and still meet our goals.

❖ We are willing to take responsibility for the quality and depth of our communication.

❖ We have a healthy intolerance for gossip, back-biting, and negativity.

❖ We do not assume to know the intentions behind each other's words or actions until we ask.

❖ We avoid using blame to deflect our responsibility for direct communication.

❖ When we have a disagreement with another team member, we will go immediately to that person to clear the air.

❖ When we communicate together, we will focus on:
  • Issues, situations and tasks, not on persons
  • Observable behaviors and events
  • The here and the now
  • Specifics rather than generalities

❖ If we cannot resolve a conflict ourselves, we will schedule time to meet with our manager or another appropriate third party to help us work through our issues.

❖ We are willing to forgive one another when our imperfect communication results in misunderstandings and/or hurt feelings.

❖ We will hold one another accountable for the above principles and guidelines.

purpose is to focus on one pressing issue (e.g., staffing, scheduling, benefits) or one area of the organization (e.g., marketing, operations, IT, HR) that needs immediate attention.

Participants must be prepared and willing to do the following:

1. Toot their own or their team's horn about something they recently implemented that made a difference to the organization. (Starting your summit by focusing on innovations sets the tone for the entire event.)

2. Share ideas and seek solutions rather than focus on problems.

These constitute your "ground rules."

❖ THE PROCESS

*   Begin your summit by clearly defining the issue or area on your agenda. Common sense dictates that clearly understanding a problem leads to clearer solutions. Therefore, ask participants to offer their perceptions and agree on the real obstacles to be hurdled.

*   Set up solutions teams with facilitators, note takers, and reporters. Decide beforehand the best way to configure teams to maximize the

creative flow of ideas; for example, form teams from a mix of generations, departments, or disciplines. Ask members not only to suggest innovative ways to resolve problems but also to prioritize their suggestions, defining deadlines, parameters, and implementers.

- Instruct note takers to record all the suggestions generated by their teams. After the summit, these must be emailed to a designated staffer, who will then synthesize and distribute them immediately so no one's ideas are lost. The fact is, what may not work today may be exactly the innovation you need tomorrow.

- Return to the large-group format and ask the reporters to discuss their team's priorities. After everyone hears the solutions, ask participants to prioritize those they are ready and willing to implement immediately. What other ideas and strategies must be added to the plan? What are the deadlines and parameters? Who are the parties accountable for implementation?

- Publicize the solutions and the actions that will be implemented along with idea-owners, imple-menters, and deadlines. Offer incentives to those individuals and/or teams who successfully implement the best time-, money-, and energy-saving solutions.

The most effective innovations in every organization often come from the "trenches"—from the people who face a problem or frustration every day. Innovation summits, then, are another vehicle to facilitate communication among your people, empowering them to clear away the obstacles that have an adverse impact on their work.

BEST PRACTICE 21: Create an Environment That Encourages Courtesy, Kindness and Respect

A fortysomething told us: "I had a boss for over a year who never said 'Good morning,' 'Good night,' or 'How was your weekend?' He basically ignored me. We never had staff meetings or one-on-one meetings. He never gave me any unsolicited feedback on my work. This manager did hire me, not inherit me."

Ouch! Such behavior isn't just discourteous, it's downright disrespectful. Contrast that experience to one of another fortysomething, who described her manager this way: "She was 10 years older than I, and she was very friendly with everybody. Very conscious of her well-being, she was also conscious of others. . . . She worked with us as adults, not condescendingly. I felt I wouldn't be cast aside if I made a mistake. . . . We shared the same huge office, so I could hear her phone conversations. She was as respectful with her boss as she was with her friends and family. She could disagree, and she did; but her respect for human beings was a strong value, and it showed everywhere."

Now that's more like it. Every member of every generation wants to be respected; everyone, regardless of age, deserves courteous treatment. How do courtesy, kindness, and respect permeate *your* team's just-in-time communication?

We went to people-performance specialist Shawna Schuh to find out how these behaviors play out in a multigenerational workplace. Shawna explained that today "the rule is to break all the rules. The only challenge is that many people don't even know the rules. Or maybe one generation knows them and another generation doesn't. That can lead to upsetting miscommunication."

She added: "The only way this challenge can be overcome is to go back to a few basics that aren't so much about strict etiquette rules, but more about good old-fashioned kindness. This will keep the courtesy going and generational mixes more productive and profitable."

How can people of all ages show courtesy, kindness, and respect to one another? Shawna recommends eight winning practices:

1. Call people by their formal name when meeting them for the first time, unless you are introduced

to them by their first name. It's always a safe bet to err on the side of formality and wait until they invite informality.

2. Introduce all individuals—no matter who they are—whenever they join your business or social circle. This graciousness shows people you value them.

3. Be the first to offer a handshake. This small act of courtesy breaks invisible barriers, makes important connections, and conveys "Welcome! I'm open to engage in conversation with you!"

4. Say "please" and "thank you." These often-forgotten words of courtesy are vital to showing respect and appreciation.

5. Ask others if you can get them something while you're up or while you're out: a cup of coffee, a lunch order, office supplies, whatever. This act of kindness assures people you are thinking of them as well as yourself.

6. Pick up after yourself so others don't have to. This is a kindness no one will notice until you don't do it. Then it will not only be noticed, but talked about and resented.

7. Keep gossip or hurtful information to yourself. This is one of the most beneficial best practices for everyone. Gossip is not kind.

8. Ask before you take someone's time. No matter how important you feel your information is, no matter how much you know it will help the other person, *ask* before launching into it. This extends kindness to others, shows respect for their time, and demonstrates that you're etiquette-savvy.

A fortysomething made this plea for courtesy: "I'd like to see people of all generations be more polite and more aware of others. . . . Anyone can say "please," "thank you," or "pardon me" and be considered courteous. Such behavior reduces the contentiousness of every-day life and allows us to operate effectively."

Mutual respect is exhibited through thoughtful, kind, courteous behaviors. Model, teach, and expect these behaviors from everyone, regardless of age. They will maximize the positive impact of your team's just-in-time communication.

For a review of our "best practices" for communication, see next page.

BEST PRACTICES

8. *Seize informal timeout times.*

9. *Establish formal timeout times.*

10. *Circulate everyone's to-do lists.*

11. *Publicize weekly accomplishments.*

12. *Create unique email subject lines.*

13. *Encourage members to ask for help.*

14. *Create an experts database.*

15. *Create a shared-notes system.*

16. *Hit the ground running with action-packed meetings.*

17. *Evaluate team effectiveness.*

18. *Evaluate the effectiveness of individual team members.*

19. *Help teams create conflict-resolution guidelines.*

20. *Call an innovation summit quarterly or biannually.*

21. *Create an environment that encourages courtesy, kindness, and respect.*

Chapter 6.

Customize! Customize! Customize!

AN 80-YEAR-OLD master butcher negotiates a 15-hour workweek with a neighborhood meat market. He teaches his specialized skills to young non-English-speaking workers. "We use our own sign language," he laughs. "It works fine."

A 72-year-old retiree from the heavy-equipment industry recently returns from a three-week project in Australia. His former employer has lured him back after six years of retirement. They know that his expertise in setting up financial systems far surpasses that of their present employees.

A 50-year-old retired fire chief who owns a management-training business posts his resume online. Within 10 minutes he receives a call from a fire-equipment distributor looking for a regional sales manager. He negotiates a telecommuting work arrangement, a signing bonus of a month's salary, flexible vacation time, and the chance to promote his training business throughout the company's sales territory.

If you think free agency is only a short-term Gen X phenomenon, think again. It's already mainstream in the free market of multi-generational talent. Skilled and talented individuals of all ages will always be up for grabs—and they know it. They're looking for options and opportunities for learning, growing, adding value, and receiving recognition. If they can find those within your organization, great. You have a strategic advantage over your competitors. If not, they'll go elsewhere, taking your training and expertise along with them.

As we said earlier, the traditional value of loyalty to an organization, espoused by Veterans and Silents, has been transformed by younger generations (including a growing number of Boomers) into loyalty to one's career and life.

Even when people insist they are loyal to their employers, their actions belie their words.

One day we were talking to a 24-year-old financial advisor who had just jumped from one firm to its competitor across town. When we mentioned that we do ongoing research on his generation, he snapped, "Oh, I'm not an Xer. I believe in loyalty and paying my dues."

"But you just told us you job-hopped," we said.

"Of course," he replied brusquely. "I got a better deal."

*"I am loyal to my employer **until** I get a better deal."*
That's the new paradigm. We call it "just-in-time loyalty."
And it's espoused by workers of all ages riding the free-agency wave.

Customize Everything You Can

The best strategy to win the just-in-time loyalty of the best talent in every generation is to customize every aspect of the employer-employee relationship. When it comes to scheduling, compensation, incentives, training, or advancement, "one size fits all" doesn't work.

Obviously, people have needs that differ from one stage of life to another. They also hold different "equity positions" on your team in terms of time, talent, contribution, enthusiasm, innovation, knowledge, skills, and results. Your goal, then, is to treat them equitably. The more customized bargaining chips you have at your disposal, the more equitable you can be and the more access you'll have to their just-in-time loyalty.

This chapter provides you with four best practices for effectively customizing everything you can. Once again, we have numbered these practices as additions to those presented earlier.

Best Practices: Customization

BEST PRACTICE 22: Let Everyone Know What's on the Table

Many organizations suffer from the proverbial problem of the left hand not knowing what the right hand is doing. At managers' meetings, we often hear comments like "I didn't know we had that benefit. I didn't know we could do that!" One manager almost lost a valued staffer because he was unaware of his company's extensive maternity-leave benefits until he heard about them from another department.

As a Gen Mix manager, you must know not only what your organization offers to attract the best talent, but also what flexibility you have to customize work arrangements. Talk to other managers. What are they doing? What have they tried to do? How are they pushing the envelope of their authority to create customized arrangements that work for the individual, the team, and the organization? What innovations are you willing to try today? Tomorrow? Next week?

Communicate "what's on the table" to your *present* employees, not just your new hires. Level the playing field and negotiate equitably with each individual. In the process, you'll eliminate the myriad of conflicts that arise over the issue of fairness.

A Case Study

Let's eavesdrop on a multi-generational conversation that could take place on any Friday afternoon in any organization in any part of the country.

"Wait a minute, Cynthia. Where are you going?" a 50-year-old says, looking up from his desk. "You're not leaving, are you? It's only three. We don't close until five-thirty."

"My kids have soccer games on Fridays, John, and I want to be there," the 33-year-old new staffer responds. "This was the arrangement I asked for when I signed on, and this is what Jeff agreed to. I negotiated for what I need."

"That's not fair," chimes in a 59-year-old. "I've been here for 15 years and I can't just up and leave."

"What's not fair," a 21-year-old counters, "is treating everyone the same when we all produce results at a different pace. If I can reach my goals in two days and it takes you three, why should I have to put in more time? I should have Fridays off!"

Imagine you are Jeff, the Gen Mix manager. How will you clear the air with your team on Monday morning and get them back on track, working collaboratively?

BEST PRACTICE 23: Offer Incentives That Have "Three-F Appeal"

In our work with various industries, we have found that incentives and rewards based on the three F's—family, fun, and flexibility—are among the most popular of bargaining chips. How creative are you in each of these areas?

❖ FAMILY APPEAL

- A managing director at TLP, a Dallas-based marketing agency, told us about his company's family advocacy program, TLParents. He explained that the program "sponsors in-house Halloween trick-or-treat parties for kids and arranges time off for parents to attend parent/teacher conferences or take their youngsters to doctors' appointments. Overall, the program makes sure that being an employee [at TLP] doesn't exclude being a parent too."

- Childcare was a top priority for the 120 young staffers at a small ad agency in southern California. After listening to their needs, the agency discovered that the staffers were willing to contribute $150 a week per family for onsite childcare. Consequently, it hired one teacher for every four youngsters, and provided playpens in offices so parents could spend lunchtime with their children. The result? High morale and high productivity and retention rates.

- Boomers who have grown children don't need childcare. Their growing concern is eldercare. In fact, according to corporate gerontologist and President of The SpeakEasy Group, Ellen Eichelbaum, "eldercare has taken over childcare as the number one problem in our workplace today. Companies will have no choice but to address the issues of their employees' dealing with eldercare stress." Eichelbaum reports that "within the next five years, almost two out of four employees will have this problem. The bottom line is poor attendance (up to 46 days per year are lost due to eldercare), reduced job productivity, decrease in job satisfaction and focus, poor attitude, and early involuntary retirement. This is no longer a choice for the employer."

  Whether you offer Boomers information about eldercare facilities and estate planning or give them flexibility to take parents to doctors' appointments and to do weekly shopping, find innovative ways to address an issue that will become even more critical for Boomers during the next decade.

- Many organizations ensure that families consistently know how much they appreciate members.

Some send letters of appreciation, flowers, or restaurant gift certificates to employees' homes to thank supportive families. One even rewarded a spouse with a gift certificate to a luxurious spa. Why? Because her husband had just returned from three productive weeks on the road and the company wanted to recognize her for taking on all the family duties while he was away.

- Businesses from credit unions to bookstores offer pick-up laundry services for their employees so there's one less chore for them to do at home. One elementary school even installed a washer and dryer onsite as an incentive for parent volunteers.

- After hiring a Gen Y college grad for her large Midwestern bank, an HR director sent a letter home to the grad's parents, expressing her delight at having him on board and complimenting him on his interviewing skills. She invited the parents to visit the bank to see the environment in which he would be working and to meet his manager and coworkers.

❖ FUN APPEAL

- There's virtually no limit to what organizations will do to energize their teams with fun—and usually low-cost—activities.

- Everyone loves food and the socializing that comes with it. Some organizations offer "Bagel Wednesdays," "Popcorn Thursdays," or "Ice Cream Social Fridays" as ongoing events.

  Others sponsor ethnic-food potlucks as a way to celebrate diversity as well as bring people together. One company even published a diversity cookbook with easy-to-use recipes and educational pieces about their origins.

- Throw "wind downs": one-time events to celebrate the end of a project or stressful stretch of time. These might include onsite parties, trips to sporting events or amusement parks, or team lunches at a favorite restaurant.

- Maximize the talent within your talent.

  For example, one Boomer manager explained to us what she did when a staffer showed talent in an area outside her job description: "I allowed this talent to bloom, and we were both rewarded with a sense of growth. Mine was noticing an emerging talent and hers was noticing a talent she did not know she had. I will never forget the sense that something bigger was happening here."

  "Something bigger" can happen when you realize that the people working with you every day are not only engineers, designers, nurses, accountants, salespeople, or telemarketers, but also poets, painters, photographers, dancers, musicians, songwriters, storytellers, athletes, landscapers, and fine-cuisine chefs. They have all kinds of talents that could add richness to your environment.

Finding that talent and letting it shine within the world of work gives people of all ages a chance to see others in a completely new light. Take the manager who was about to hire a professional photographer to illustrate a new brochure. In the course of an informal chat, he discovered that one of his staffers was an amateur photographer. He asked to see the young man's work, and was so impressed with its quality that he hired him to "moonlight" on the project.

Such talent can be used for charitable purposes, too. For example, some organizations collaborate with groups like the United Way to sponsor fundraising talent shows that put their own people in the spotlight. We at RainmakerThinking work with a nonprofit organization that holds an annual coffeehouse where people of all ages share their music, poetry, and visual art.

The fact is, the talent within your talent can generate excitement and enthusiasm that spills over into everyday collaboration and productivity. How can you unleash it so "something bigger" happens on your team?

- Appoint a "fun raiser" and give him or her a catchy title like "The Pharaoh of Fun." (Ben and Jerry's calls theirs "Granter o' Wishes.") Create a fun budget and give your fun raiser the responsibility to get everyone involved in how the budget is used. Since what is "fun" for one person may be drudgery for another, the more choices you offer, the more likely it is that people will find an activity custom-fit for what they enjoy.

❖ FLEXIBILITY APPEAL

- Remember that time is a valuable commodity. In fact, most people tell us that time is more important to them than money.

  The Director of a VA hospital recounted that he gave a $2500 bonus to a staffer who had successfully completed an exceptionally difficult assignment. He was surprised to see her in his office within hours. "I'm going to give this back to you," she said, handing him the check. "I'd like to have a week off in September instead to spend time with my family."

  "That $2500 was worth more than two weeks of her salary," the Director explained, "but time off was more valuable to her. I agreed to give it to her."

One of our interviewees added she is even willing to give back nine percent of her salary to work from home. "The nine percent," she told us, "represents approximately how much I spend monthly for gas, meals out due to lack of time to prepare them, and someone to do my family's laundry every week. I believe I can realistically perform my job duties from home."

- Be creative at negotiating time off and flexible scheduling as incentives. Here are three of the most effective tactics we've discovered:

  — Issue "Take-a-Day" certificates redeemable within 90 days. It entitles the bearer to a day off as a reward for producing extraordinary results.

  — Offer summer (or other seasonal) flex hours when business slows down. Some companies offer a choice of five paid Fridays off during the summer; others close their offices at 3 p.m. each Friday. Some organizations completely close down between Christmas and New Year's Day, making it a mandatory vacation time for everyone. Since their clients are too involved in holiday activities to need extensive services, it makes sense to let employees enjoy the holidays without the stress of work.

— Offer holiday work-volunteer opportunities. In some industries, like healthcare and retail, working on holidays is imperative. Before you go through the hassle of trying to schedule holidays equitably, why not give team members the opportunity to volunteer to work? The payoff? In addition to time and a half (or whatever monetary bonus you offer), give them an extra paid day (or two!) off for each holiday worked. Since holidays have different value and meaning to different people, you may be pleasantly surprised to discover the trade-offs staffers are willing to make for that kind of incentive.

BEST PRACTICE 24: Set Up Career Development Accounts

This is a no-brainer. You have to customize training to meet the needs of your age-diverse team. It's true that most people in every generation prefer the hands-on, practical approach to training, where there is a clear relationship between what they're learning and how they'll use it. It's also true that older generations prefer classroom-style training, where they can interact with an instructor and with one another, while many Xers and Yers prefer the self-paced, independent-study style of computer-based training. Online education is great for some workers; it's a turnoff for others.

Through a savvy HR professional, we discovered an innovative tool for managing this situation. It's called the career development account (CDA). The professional defined CDAs as "budgeted training dollars allocated to individuals to use according to broad guidelines." She explained, "We generally approve expenditures on any-thing related to self-development because we believe that all development enhances performance in some way."

If classes in yoga or tai chi facilitate relaxation and focus, how appropriate for the workplace! If classes in literature, art or music expand the imagination and touch the spirit, why not? Offer your people the opportunity to customize their self-development, and watch how it maximizes their performance.

BEST PRACTICE 25: Customize Leadership Opportunities

One of the biggest challenges young managers face is gaining the respect of older workers. A savvy VP of Accounting at an international marketing firm told us he tackles this issue by "test driving" potential new man-agers before handing out any promotions.

"We have them lead a variety of project teams before we move them into management," he explained. "This gives them a chance to see how well they like managing other people, as well as lets us observe how others react to their leadership. If they are promoted, they walk into the position with much more visibility and credibility."

Start by giving people with management potential the opportunity to lead team meetings, head up projects, present training sessions, and attend important business functions with you or as your representative. Make them visible. Give them as many chances to hone their interpersonal skills as you can find before you promote them.

When someone is promoted, immediately set him or her up with a coach—a highly successful manager who can guide them through the initial challenges of this new "profession." Management is indeed a profession all its own. It requires talents, skills, and behaviors that go far beyond whatever technical expertise a person already has. The biggest mistake organizations make is expecting great technicians to become great managers automatically. That's the formula for disaster.

Recognize that sometimes the worst way to reward people is to promote them to management. In such cases, you're faced with a different set of challenges: What other bargaining chips do you have at your disposal to recognize them? How can you raise their status in your organization and reward their contributions without putting them in a box on a chart that may stifle their talents? How expert have you become at customizing incentives?

❖ Review ...

BEST PRACTICES

22. *Let everyone know what's on the table.*

23. *Offer incentives that have "three-F appeal."*

24. *Set up career development accounts.*

25. *Customize leadership opportunities.*

In Conclusion . . .

PEOPLE OFTEN ASK US: "Haven't generations always been in conflict with one another? What's the big deal? It's always been like this and it always will be."

That's true—intergenerational power struggles and coming-of-age conflicts are certainly part of the human condition. However, in terms of the workplace, today's generational issues are unique, transcending traditional parent-child or sibling clashes. They reflect the challenges businesses are having as they struggle to move out of the workplace of the past into that of the future.

Every generation is now living through the most profound changes in the economy since the Industrial Revolution, and each is responding differently. Silents are asking, "Where are the good old days of job security, company loyalty, and people willing to pay their dues?" Boomers are complaining, "We've finally arrived and now everything is changing. How do we adapt without losing our hard-won status? How do we get the respect we deserve?" Xers are wondering, "What's the big deal? It was like this when we got here, and we like it." Yers are exclaiming, "We're going to be successful professionals doing meaningful work with great team players!"

Whatever the response, the fact is, everyone, regardless of age, is a member of the workforce of the future. Everyone, regardless of generation, must become flexible, entrepreneurial, techno-savvy knowledge workers focused on getting great work done—or risk becoming obsolete. This is the common ground on which everyone must collaborate, and on which you must manage.

The New "Gen Mixers"

People of all ages have already started to dissolve the boundaries between generations as they adapt to the new workplace. A 52-year-old manager in direct-mail advertising boasts that his coworkers call him a "Boom X" because of his free-agency mindset. A 41-year-old Social Services office manager explains, "I'm not sure of my generation, and overall I feel it doesn't really matter. I started as a Boomer and have *evolved* into X—and possibly Y" (emphasis ours).

The vice-president of a large outplacement corporation confides, "After many changes in my career, I have learned to be more Gen X at 50 than anyone. You see, after being raised by parents of the 1950s, I was told to find a good job, learn to type, and the rest will come. Leaving with the plaques and recognition after 30 years was supposed to be my goal. Well, it doesn't work that way. The way it works is to be up on the latest, be willing to change, be enthusiastic, articulate, and knowledge-able about technology. If you can't talk it, you won't be able to walk it!"

We couldn't have said it better! That's "the way it works" for people of every generation. The most successful people in the twenty-first century, then, will be true "Gen Mixers," people of all ages who bring to work every day their enthusiasm, flexibility, and voracious desire to learn. They may or may not have memories of World War II or Watergate. They may or may not have experi-enced command-and-control leadership or pay-your-dues ladder climbing. They may or may not have been latchkey kids or techno-whizzes. What they will be, however, is 100 percent responsible for how they cre-ate their lives and how they use their talents and skills to collaborate on getting the best work done every day.

There's no doubt about it: That's the kind of team any manager would love to lead. And that's what you can look forward to as you bridge the understanding gap, master the competencies of focus, communication, and customization, and steer your team away from collision toward collaboration.

— *Postscript* —

This book was in the hands of our editor when the events of September 11, 2001, united generations of Americans in ways we never could have anticipated. As we watched and prayed with our country and our world, we wondered as authors if we needed to rethink our research or revise our recommendations. After careful scrutiny, our conclusion was "no." The major themes of our work are even more important today.

The skills, talents, and expertise of every generation are needed more than ever to rebuild an economy that has been on a rollercoaster ride for nearly two decades.

The orderly, predictable world of strategic plans, organization charts, and job descriptions had disappeared long before the World Trade Center was attacked. In an unstable, unpredictable world, organizations must turn diversity into a strength and become fluid and flexible to meet marketplace demands.

"The work" of an organization is the common ground that unites every generation. Now this work extends beyond day-to-day tasks, into the larger arena of healing and building lasting relationships. "Just-in-time loyalty" must be earned every day by organizations, managers, and coworkers.

An HR professional in New York City told us, "I only hope that businesses finally get the message: People are their most important asset."

We second that hope.

Recommended Resources

Barnett, Dick. *Re-Ignite Your Business: The Secret of Leading with Confidence, Ease, and Certainty.* Beaverton, OR: Confident Leader Press, 1997.

Eichelbaum, Ellen. See www.speakeasygroup.com.

Foot, David K., and Daniel Stoffman. *Boom, Bust and Echo 2000: Profiting from the Demographic Shift in the New Millennium.* Toronto: Stoddart Publishing, 2000.

Goldberg, Beverly. *Age Works: What Corporate America Must Do to Survive the Graying of the Workforce.* New York: Free Press, 2000.

Hicks, Kathy, and Rick Hicks. *Boomers, Xers, and Other Strangers: Understanding the Generational Differences That Divide Us.* Colorado Springs, CO: Focus on the Family Pub, 1999.

Martin, Carolyn A., and Bruce Tulgan. *Managing Generation Y: Global Citizens Born in the Late Seventies and Early Eighties.* Amherst, MA: HRD Press, 2001.

Schuh, Shawna. *How to Out-Finesse the Competition: 324 Get-Ahead Ideas and Business Skills.* Digital book (www.BusinessGraces.com).

Smith, J. Walker, and Ann S. Clurman. *Rocking the Ages: The Yankelovich Report on Generational Marketing.* New York: Harperbusiness, 1997.

Stillman, David, and Lynne Lancaster. *When Generations Collide: Who They Are, Why They Clash, How to Solve the Generational Puzzle at Work.* New York: HarperCollins, 2002.

Strauss, William, and Neil Howe. *Generations: The History of America's Future, 1584 to 2069.* New York: William Morrow & Co, 1992.

Tapscott, Don. *Growing Up Digital: The Rise of the Net Generation.* New York: McGraw-Hill, 1998.

Thau, Richard D., and Jay S. Heflin, eds. *Generations Apart: Xers vs. Boomers vs. the Elderly* (Contemporary Issues series). Amherst, NY: Prometheus Books, 1997.

Tulgan, Bruce. *Managing Generation X: How to Bring Out the Best in Young Talent.* Revised ed. New York: W. W. Norton & Company, 2000.

Tulgan, Bruce. *The Manager's Pocket Guide to Generation X.* Amherst, MA: HRD Press, 1997.

Zemke, Ron, Claire Raines, and Bob Filipczak. *Generations at Work: Managing the Clash of Veterans, Boomers, Xers, and Nexters in Your Workplace.* New York: AMACOM, 1999.